It's Not Fai

CONTENTS

CONTENTS

TO SET THE SCENE:

CHRISTIAN AID/SUNIL GUPTA

PROPHECY OF AN ASIAN WOMAN

All the broken hearts
shall rejoice;
all those
who are heavy laden,
whose eyes are tired
and do not see,
shall be lifted up
to meet with the healer.
The battered souls and bodies
shall be healed;
the hungry
shall be fed;
the imprisoned
shall be free;
all earthly children
shall regain joy
in the reign
of the just and loving one
coming for you,
coming for me
in this time,
in this world.

Sun Ai Lee Park, South Korean theologian

Acknowledgements

This book was produced on behalf of the youth departments of Christian Aid, CAFOD and SCIAF as a resource for youth groups.

Based on original text by Anne Wilkinson-Hayes, author of the first edition of *It's Not Fair*.

Written and compiled by Jim Walton.

Edited by Judy Rogers and Jonathan Smith, Christian Aid Youth Education Advisers.

With grateful thanks to Barbara Crowther and Helen Connor.

Design and layout Shân Rees; sub-editor Sue Turner.

Printed by Stanley Hunt Printers Ltd, Rushden.

ISBN 0-904379-18-3

INTRODUCTION

The original *It's not Fair* was published in 1985. Its winning blend of role plays, simulation games, quizzes, ideas of working for change and much more, soon established it as a best-selling resource for youth leaders - especially those wanting to work with their groups on issues of global injustice and Third World development.

This new edition has been completely revised and updated - reflecting just how much the world has changed since the days of the Berlin Wall.

However, while many of the issues are different, this book stays true to the ideals of the original by using as wide a range of educational techniques as possible. We still believe that young people are more likely to learn if they are enjoying themselves, so all the exercises are designed to be fun as well as thought provoking.

DEVON AND CORNWALL NEWSPAPERS

Who is the book for?

It's not Fair is aimed primarily at leaders of groups of young people aged 14 and over. However, with a little thought, many of the exercises can be adapted for younger groups.

The book is written from an ecumenical Christian perspective and includes Christian reflections and Bible studies. Where biblical references are made the Jerusalem Bible has often been used. Much of it, nonetheless, will work with secular groups or those of other faiths.

How to use the book

It's not Fair can be used in a number of ways. The 19 chapters form a sequence which can be used as a complete course, or you can dip into the book as and when appropriate. For weekend conferences or sessions lasting longer than an evening, you should ideally use at least one programme from each of the three sections: Values, Issues and Taking Action; you should certainly include some of the 'Taking Action' material from the third.

JOANNE O'BRIEN/FORMAT

Other points to bear in mind:

- **The timings for each exercise are somewhat approximate. If your group enjoys discussions you could allow more time.**

- **Suggested questions for discussion are given throughout the book. Feel free to use only those you think will interest your group, and to make up your own.**

■ **Photocopying of this book for group use is strictly allowed and, for some exercises, essential. Permission must be sought to reproduce materials for other purposes.**

■ **We have used the phrase 'the Third World' throughout, in preference to possibly more ideologically sound alternatives (like 'the South'). This is simply because it's the phrase most recognisable to young people.**

The Structure of the Book

ICEBREAKERS	For groups who don't know each other, some games to help to break down barriers.
VALUES	Chapters 1-4 aim to help young people think about their own values and expectations in life.
ISSUES	Chapters 5-13 are concerned with specific issues related to development and suggest how they can best be explored.
ACTION	Chapters 14-19 give lots of ideas about action you might take and plenty of practical hints for carrying it out.

The book ends with a list of resources and addresses you might find helpful.

Happy wrongs – righting!

MAGGIE MURRAY/FORMAT

Icebreakers

AIM

To break down quickly barriers between a group of people; especially valuable with people who don't know each other

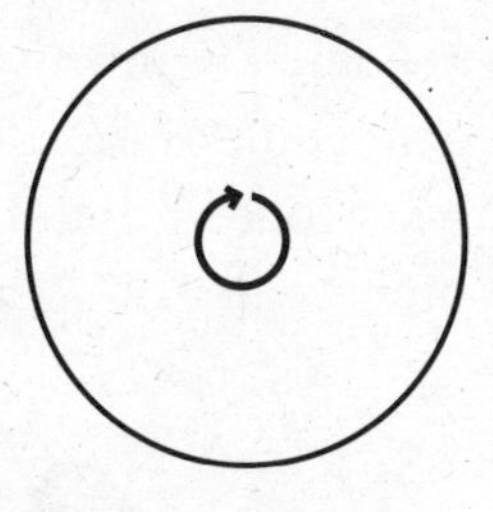

TIME
(45-60 minutes)

Choose a few suitable exercises from the following list; be sure to use at least one from each section so the personal contact builds up.

INSTRUCTIONS

■ ***Explain to the group that you are going to do some icebreaking exercises, and that for these to work you need everybody to agree to do whatever you ask them. In return, you promise not to single out or embarrass any individuals, and not to ask them to do anything physically difficult.***

■ ***Once this agreement is given, ask everyone, when you say 'Go', to push any chairs back against the walls, take off their shoes and sit on their own anywhere in the room. Shout 'Go!'***

Imagination exercises:

1

'RELAXATION'

Ask everybody to lie on their backs, not touching anyone else, and to follow these instructions:

"Close your eyes and relax... check around your body... if you find anywhere tense, relax it . . . listen to the sound of your own breathing . . . try and feel your heart beat . . .

"In a moment I will clap my hands; this will represent the alarm clock going off in the morning. When you hear it, you should 'wake up' and have a good stretch. Remember to concentrate on carrying out my instructions; don't think about anybody else." CLAP.

"Now imagine that in front of you is a large and unusually juicy orange. Try to peel it and take a segment. Imagine this as vividly as possible . . . You should now feel your hands covered in sticky orange juice. Luckily, a stream is flowing beside you and there is soap and a towel. Clean up.

"Now in front of you are some all-in-one overalls, made of paper. Put these on as carefully as possible; try not to tear them! By now you should be standing up."

2

'IMAGINATION'

Ask people to move around the room in different ways: as waiters; as small people with very large dogs on a lead; as old people; as if the floor was made of hot coals etc.

'Getting to know you' exercises:

1

'HELLO'

Ask participants to introduce themselves: first the 'British'way (shaking hands and exchanging names); then the 'Eskimo' way (rubbing noses); finally the 'French' way (kisses on both cheeks).

2

'WHO AM I?'

Ask participants to sit in a circle. Explain that you are now going to call out some categories of people. Anyone belonging to a particular category must move quickly to sit in the middle of the circle. If they belong to the next category mentioned they should stay there. Otherwise, they must quickly rejoin the circle. Possible categories include: people with pets - people with bikes - people who play a musical instrument - people who have been to Spain - people who have been to the USA - people who have been to Blackpool - people with 3 or more brothers/sisters - only children . . .

'AND ON MY LEFT . . .'

Ask people to make a big circle, then give them one minute to find out whom they are sitting next to. Go around the circle, asking each person in turn to introduce the person on their left and say something they have just learnt about them (eg: "This is Katie and she's been to Spain.")

'FILL THE GAP'

Ask everyone to sit in a circle on the floor leaving a person-sized gap. The person on the left of the gap should then shout out: "I want 'X' (name of another participant) to sit on my right." 'X' moves quickly to the gap and the new person with a gap on their right calls for someone to fill it. This continues as slickly as possible until you feel most people's names have been called. Finish the exercise by asking people to go back to their original positions.

Trust Games:

■ Ask the group to divide into pairs, find a space on the floor and sit opposite each other. Ideally, the pairs should be people who don't know each other and of different genders. For the next set of exercises people should ignore the other pairs and concentrate just on their partner.

'LISTENING'

Tell the pairs to decide which of them is going to be number 1 and which number 2. Ask the 1s to put their hands over their mouths and leave them there. Ask the 2s to explain to their partners what they most like to do in their spare time. Swap over and repeat.

'MY KINDA MUSIC'

Ask the pairs to chat about their favourite music without making eye contact. Repeat, this time staring at each other.

'TELL ALL ABOUT IT'

Next say that 1s must tell 2s animatedly something they are really excited about. The 2s, meanwhile, must completely ignore what is being said to them. Swap roles and repeat.

'MIRROR MIRROR . . .'

Explain that 1s are mirrors and 2s have just got up in the morning. The 2s go to their mirrors and do whatever they do first thing - actions which, of course, the mirrors faithfully reflect. After a few minutes 2s become the mirrors. The 1s are going out for the evening and want to look their best; they prepare in front of the mirrors...

'TRUST ME'

Announce that both partners can't hear or speak, so the exercise must be done in silence. The pairs must now sit back-to-back and link arms. Without breaking the link, they must stand up. Once they are standing, announce that the 2s are also blind and must close their eyes and be led around the room by their partner. Then reverse roles.

'LEAN ON ME'

Ask the pairs to stand facing each other, toes almost touching. They should then hold hands and see how far back they can lean.

'CATCH ME'

Finally, tell the 1s to stand just in front of the 2s with both partners facing the same way. The 1s should then relax and fall back, allowing the 2s to catch them. Ask the pairs to repeat this with the gap between partners increasing each time. Then reverse roles and repeat the exercise, before asking everybody to sit down facing you.

Small group exercises:

■ **Ask people to walk round the room and when you shout out a number, to get into groups of that size. Shout out various numbers, ending with groups of 7 where possible. Then ask the groups of 7 to sit in circles on the floor.**

'SPACES'

Ask each group to occupy the smallest space it can; then, with each group member still touching at least two others, the biggest.

'STORIES'

The groups should sit back in circles. Ask each group to build up a story, going round their circle with each member saying only one word in turn. Repeat, this time with everybody saying a sentence.

'COPYCAT'

Next, ask whoever in each group started the first story to perform a simple action (a hand wave, for example). The person on their left must repeat this action and then add one of their own. Continue, with everybody in turn doing all the previous actions in order and then adding one of their own. See if the group can go around the circle twice.

'ALL SIT DOWN'

Finally, ask each group to stand in a circle, its members facing clockwise and standing very close to each other. They should then put their hands around the waist of the person in front. Everyone must then slowly bend their knees and sit down on the 'lap' of the person behind them. When (if!) this is done, ask people to put their hands up and give themselves a clap.

Whole group exercise:

The whole group must walk around the room. When you give a signal (a clap or shout, for example) people must immediately hug one other person. The last few people to do so each time are out – and must watch as the champion huggers are revealed.

Ask your newly bonded and energised group to put their shoes back on. It is time to move on to the next part of your programme . . .

1 Mine, *all* Mine?

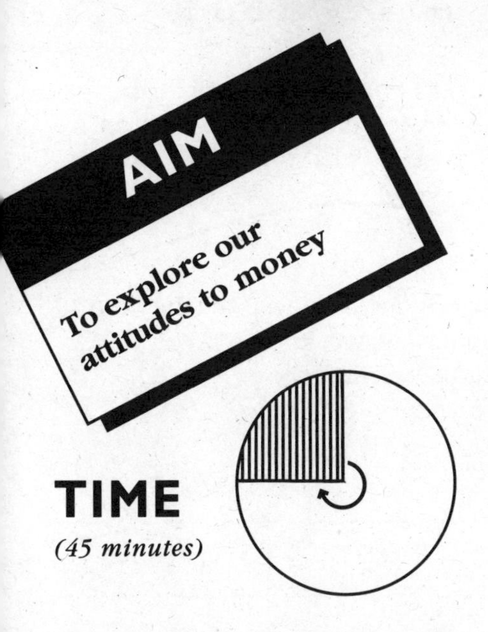

TIME
(45 minutes)

THE SITUATION

You have just found out that you have been left £400,000, after tax, by a distant relative you didn't know you had. You are also told that:

- ***You can invest the money at 10 per cent interest, but will have to pay tax at 40 per cent on the income this brings.***
- ***Because of your relative's distrust of 'youth' a trust is to be established to advise you on the management of your legacy. You must gain its approval if you wish to dispose of more than 10 per cent of your money in any one year.***

First exercise:

WHERE THERE'S A WILL . . .

papers and pens
display chart of 'The Situation'
photocopies of 'Points for Discussion'

1 Individual reactions *(5 minutes)*

- Read out and explain 'The Situation' to the group.
- Ask everyone to spend a few minutes thinking about their own reaction. (No discussion allowed at this point.)
- Encourage everybody to write down what they will do with the money.

2 Group exercise *(25 minutes)*

- Divide participants into groups of 6 or 7.
- Ask for a volunteer from each group to give his/her proposals to the group.
- The group plays the role of the trustees, discussing the proposals, asking probing questions and making recommendations.
- Meet back in the big group and see how the volunteers got on. Did they get their own way? Were the trustees trusting?

MONEY MONEY MONEY MONEY MONEY

In 2s or 3s:

■ What did you want to do with the money and why?

■ Would it make a difference to your personality?

■ Would such money change your plans for the future?

In the big group:

■ Would your attitude to the money have been different if you had found out that it had been acquired by arms trading, drug dealing, or anything else you don't approve of?

■ If it wasn't for inheritance tax on the legacy you would have received £560,000. How do you feel about the state's right to take money in this way?

■ Should being a Christian make a difference to how you decide what to do with money?

Ask group members to work out as honestly as they can how they spent their money last week. On a piece of paper fill in a grid like the following:

AMOUNT SPENT ON:

GOING OUT	SPORT	FOOD	DRINKS

CLOTHES	BOOKS	MAGAZINES	OTHER THINGS (SPECIFY)

Then ask:

■ Were you surprised by anything you found out about your spending habits?

■ It has been said that the only true way of finding out what someone really values is by seeing what they spend their money on. Do you agree?

■ Are there any differences between how you spend your money and how you thought a Christian should? (This question is not meant to be a massive guilt inducer, just gently to raise the issue taken up in the second reflection on page 12.)

40-50 minutes (including discussion)

NO MATERIALS REQUIRED

Second exercise:

SHARE AND SHARE ALIKE?

— Split the group into acting troupes of 5 or 6 people. (Fewer if necessary as you need at least two troupes.)

— Ask half the troupes to prepare and be ready to perform a sketch showing GREED; the other half a sketch showing SHARING. Allow about 20 minutes for them to create and rehearse their pieces.

— Get the whole group back together and watch the performances. Once the applause has died down, discuss with the group the following points:

■ **Did you recognise in the sketches anything of yourself, of your life, or of other people you know?**

■ **Which sketch did you relate to most, GREED or SHARING? Why was this, do you think?**

■ **Which of the sketches had happy endings? Why?**

— Show the group the charts below, read out the 'Strange but True' section and ask for reactions.

■ **Does anything in the sketches you have just seen explain such inequality?**

■ **What can be done to bring about more equality? (You may want to return to this question after doing other exercises in the book and see if it becomes easier or harder to answer.)**

■ **One way to help the charts come alive is to give out biscuits in similar proportions. Give 2 out of every 10 people 8 biscuits to share between them; the other 8 people get 2 biscuits to share. Ask them to eat the biscuits. How do they feel? You could point out that the poorest 2 in every 10 should technically have 0.1 per cent of a biscuit between them – but this would only be a crumb!**

"WHO GETS WHAT IN THE WORLD"

GROUP	Richest 20% of world population	Middle 60% of world population	Poorest 20% of world population
PERCENTAGE OF WEALTH	83%	16%	1%

World Distribution of Wealth (U.N. Development Programme Report 1992).

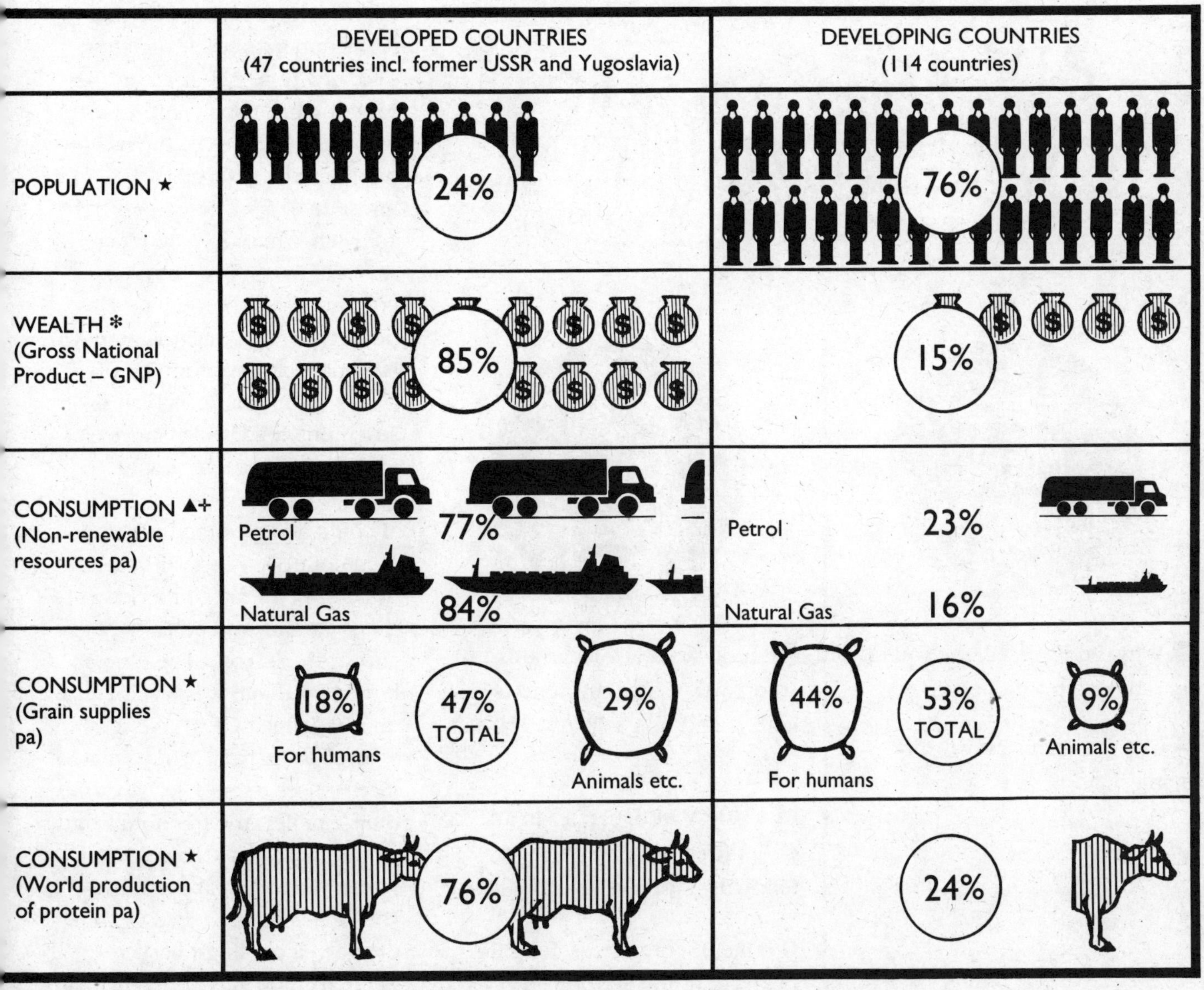

	DEVELOPED COUNTRIES (47 countries incl. former USSR and Yugoslavia)	DEVELOPING COUNTRIES (114 countries)
POPULATION ★	24%	76%
WEALTH ❄ (Gross National Product – GNP)	85%	15%
CONSUMPTION ▲+ (Non-renewable resources pa)	Petrol 77% Natural Gas 84%	Petrol 23% Natural Gas 16%
CONSUMPTION ★ (Grain supplies pa)	18% For humans 47% TOTAL 29% Animals etc.	44% For humans 53% TOTAL 9% Animals etc.
CONSUMPTION ★ (World production of protein pa)	76%	24%

A country's wealth can be conveniently reckoned as the total amount of goods and services it produces. This is called Gross National Product, or GNP.

SOURCE: ★Food and Agricultural Organisation of the United Nations (FAO UN). ❄World and Military Social Expenditures 1992.
▲BP Statistical Review of World Energy 1992. +UN Economic Survey 1992.

People in the richer countries, 23 per cent of the world's population, earn 85 per cent of the world's total income.

The richest fifth of the world's population receives 150 times the income of the poorest fifth.

The economic gap between the richest and poorest countries has doubled in the last 30 years.

UK overseas aid per head of the population is the lowest of any European country. The 1991/2 aid level of 0.32 per cent of GNP represented 3p for every £10 of government money.

(Source: United Nations Development Programme Report 1992.)

JOEL KAUFFMANN

Read Mark 10:17-31

■ Why did Jesus ask the young man to give his money away?

■ Can Christians ever justify being rich?

Read Luke 14:33

■ Can Jesus really mean this? If so, why do Christians tend to ignore it? If not, why does he say it?

■ A priest who teaches in a Catholic school tells the following story:

"I remember once teaching RE in a very bright sixth form class. We were looking at the gospel story of the rich young man. I asked the class the meaning of the story and their answers couldn't have been better. They really understood. Jesus, they said, saw how riches get in the way of what's really important, how they blind us to the needs of others; he realised the injustice of a world where there are such differences between rich and poor. But, they continued, Christ's call to poverty is not a negative one – it is actually an invitation to a far richer life in him, in which his sustaining love brings more true joy than money ever could.

"I could add nothing to their comments, so I just said: 'So none of you want to be rich then?' and moved on to the next part of the lesson. The class's howl of outrage was instant and unmistakable. Of course they wanted to be rich. They wanted nice houses, money to look after their families, the freedom from anxiety that wealth brings and so on. 'But what about what you've just been saying about the gospel reading?' I asked. Their attitude was clear: that had been religion, this was real life."

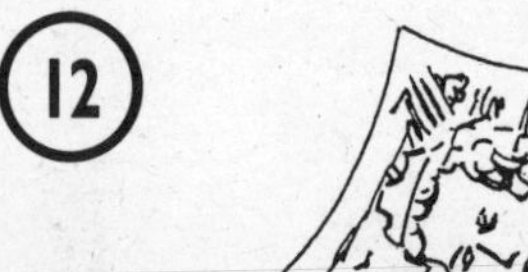

JOEL KAUFFMANN

SIGH. BIBLE STUDY WOULD BE A LOT MORE USEFUL TO ME--

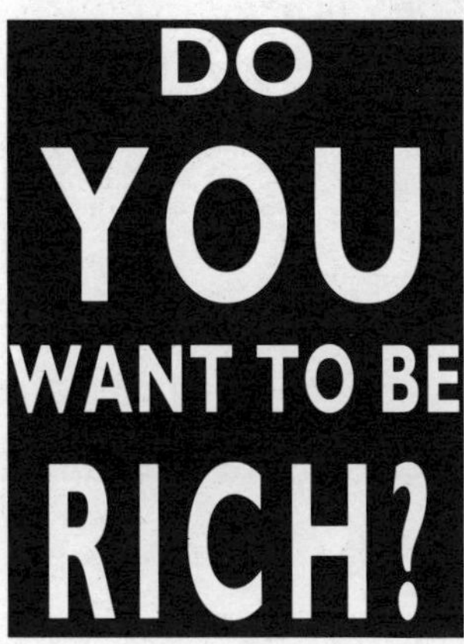

Other thoughts on WEALTH:

The earth was made for all, rich and poor, in common. Why do you rich claim it as your exclusive right?

St Ambrose (340-397 AD)

Wealth is always the result of theft, if not committed by the actual possessor, then by his predecessor.

St Jerome (340-420 AD)

I used to think when I was a child, that Christ might have been exaggerating when he warned about the dangers of wealth. Today I know better. I know how very hard it is to be rich and still keep the milk of human kindness. Money has a dangerous way of putting scales on one's eyes, a dangerous way of freezing people's hands, eyes, lips and hearts.

Dom Helder Camara, a contemporary Brazilian bishop

For though the will to do what is good is in me, the power is not: the good thing I want to do, I never do; the evil thing which I do not want – that is what I do.

Paul's letter to the Romans 7:19

JOEL KAUFFMANN

2 It's not the Winning and Losing

The first two exercises below cover the same ground. Choose the one you prefer or which seems more suited to your group (the first needs far less preparation for big groups). Try to do the third soon after.

First exercise:

FIST OR PALM?

TIME
(35 minutes)

large chart showing scoring (see below)
papers and pens

INSTRUCTIONS:

— Divide the group into pairs. Give each pair a pen and paper. Tell them the rules of the exercise and explain the scoring system. Be careful to avoid words like 'winning' or 'losing' and do not in any other way imply that this is a competitive exercise. (Though most participants will assume it is.)

RULES

- **The game is played in silence. Only the leader may speak.**
- **Partners face each other with hands hidden (under a table or behind their backs).**
- **On a given signal from the leader, players show their partner either a clenched fist or an open palm.**
- **Each pair keeps its own score.**

— When you are sure everyone understands the rules, start the game. Give a clear signal for hands to be shown. Repeat 10 times. Ask for scores. Has anyone scored more than 30? Anyone under 20? Do not comment.

— Now play the game again, but this time tell the players that they can discuss the game, negotiate possible moves with their partner and take their 10 goes in their own time. Again they record their scores. Ask for scores and begin discussion.

- Did people want to 'win'? If so, why? (It was not introduced as a competitive game.)
- Did any pairs operate differently the second time around? Why/why not? How did it work?
- Did anybody agree a move and then cheat?
- What did you learn about yourself (or your partner) from the game?
- Can you think of any real situations which are like the game, in your own life or globally?
- Is competition more fun than co-operation? In this game? Generally?
- In what ways do you think competition is a good thing? A bad thing?

Second exercise:

SQUARING UP

YOU WILL NEED **(per group of 5)**
Five 15cm squares in stiff card
5 envelopes

TIME
(30-35 minutes)

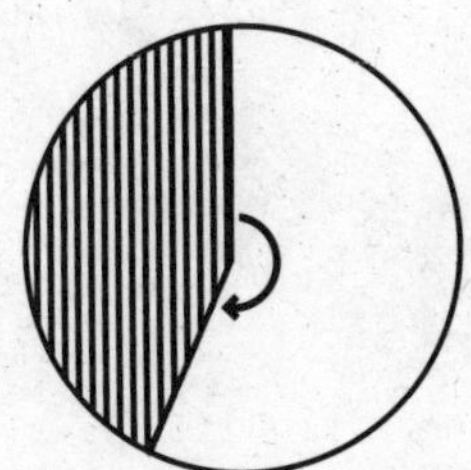

Advance preparation *(for one group of 5):*

— Rule five 15cm squares on card or stiff paper and mark as shown; be as accurate as possible.

— Cut out the shapes and sort them into sets of the same letter. Put each set in an envelope marked with the letter.

15cm

15cm

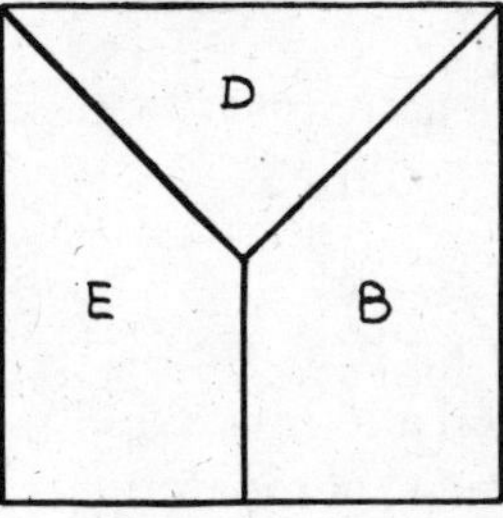

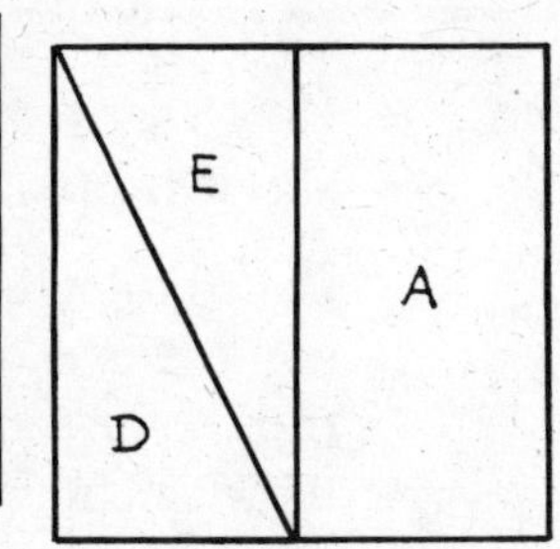

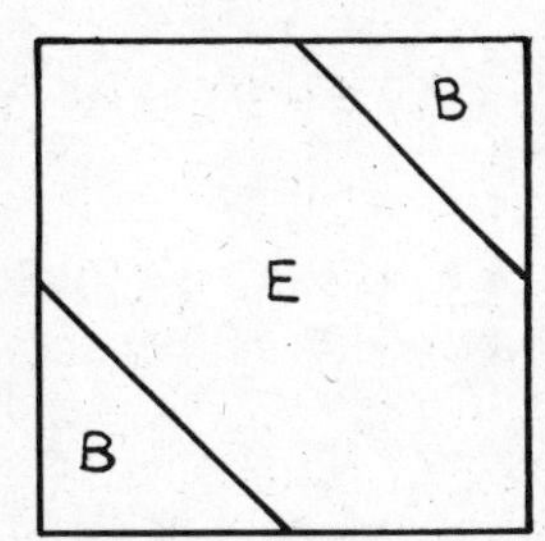

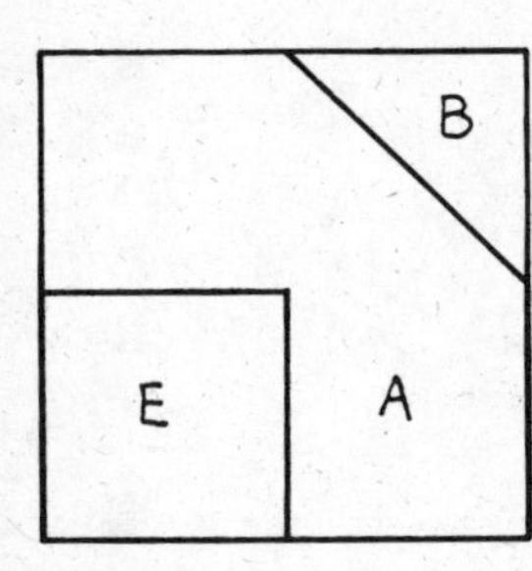

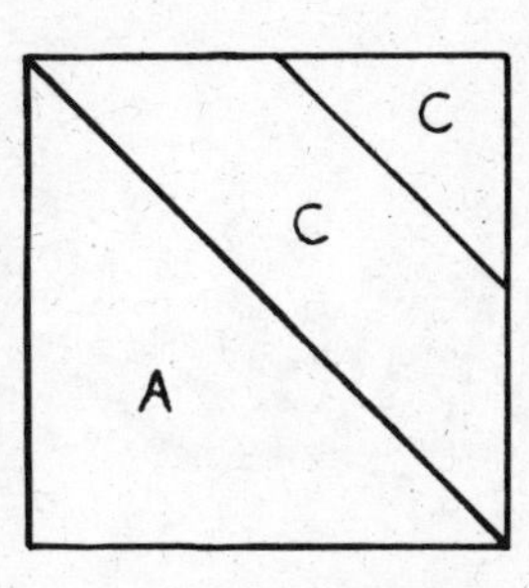

INSTRUCTIONS:

— Divide into groups of 5. (Some people may have to be spectators. They can report on what they observe.) Give everyone in a group an envelope.

— Read out or write up the following instructions.

- **On the starting signal, open the envelopes and take out the contents.**
- **The exercise will continue until each person completes a square.**
- **You may pass a piece of card to another member, but you may NOT reach out and take one.**
- **No talking or any other kind of communication is allowed.**
- **You may at any time decline to take further part.**

— Usually at least one square is formed which is not one of those illustrated. This will hold up the group until the person responsible dismantles it.

- What happened?
- What feelings did people have in the course of the game?
- Was your reaction to try and get your own square? If so, why? (It was not one of the instructions.)
- Can you see any parallels from real life with any aspects of the game?
- Is competition more fun than co-operation? In this game? Generally?
- In what ways do you think the spirit of competition is a good thing? A bad thing?

Third exercise:

WORKING TOGETHER

— Divide participants into groups of 5 or 6 and ask the groups to sit in a circle on the floor with no shoes on.

— If people don't know each other, give them a few minutes to introduce themselves and chat.

— Now tell the groups that they have to design a machine with each group member being part of it. It must be a moving machine. They now have one minute to decide what they are going to be. There must be no movement yet.

— They now have one minute to put their machine into action.

— Get everyone sitting down again. Then ask each group in turn to perform their machine for the others who have to guess what it is.

TIME

25-30 minutes)

- Was it easy to work together? Why/why not?
- Did one person take the lead? How did the others feel about this?
- How did the groups rate their machines?
- What did the activity tell you about working together?
- Did the groups feel competitive about how well they co-operated and how good their machine was, compared with other groups? If so, what does this mean?

A PROBLEM . . .

Two hundred people lived in the suburb of a large town and worked in the town centre. Each of them realised that the bus journey to work lasted half-an-hour, whereas going by car only took 15 minutes. So everybody began to go by car. Unfortunately, as a result, the roads became jammed and the journey by car began to take an hour. Frustration set in until the people held a large meeting and agreed that they would all go by bus. This went well for a while. Extra buses were laid on and everybody took 30 minutes to get to work. But then, some of the people realised something . . .

Now that everybody was going by bus the roads were nice and clear, so they could go by car in only 15 minutes. This they did. As their cars zipped by, the people still travelling by bus became resentful. Why should they be stuck on a rattly bus just to keep the roads clear for the selfish car drivers? More and more people went back to their cars and soon the roads were just as choked up as before.

- **What do you think you would have done at each point if you had been one of the suburb dwellers?**
- **What does the story say about co-operation?**
- **How can the problem be solved?**

If only people would see each other as the agents of each other's happiness, they could occupy the earth, their common habitation, in peace, and move forward confidently together to their common goal.

The prospect changes when they regard each other as obstacles; soon they have no choice left but to flee or be forever fighting. Humankind then seems nothing but a gigantic error of nature.

Abbé Sieyés, from *The Birthright of Man* edited by Alice Sullivan

In the Bible it is written that what God gave us is for us all. I often think how beautiful it would be if everyone understood this.

Prayer from Honduras

When all the people asked him (John the Baptist), "What must we do then?" he answered: "Anyone who has two tunics, he must share with the one who has none, and anyone with something to eat must do the same."

Luke 3:10-11

WE MUST SHARE

GUY PARKER REES

3 Ways of Life

First exercise:

GREAT EXPECTATIONS?

large pieces of paper
selection of felt-tips

Part A

— Split the group into 2s or 3s and ask everybody to tell their partners how they would complete the following sentences:

> **If my dreams come true, in 10 years I'll be . . .**
> **In 10 years time, I expect to be . . .**
> **If my dreams come true, in 30 years I'll be . . .**
> **In 30 years time, I expect to be . . .**
> **I'd like to be remembered as . . .**

— Back as the whole group, compare answers, then ask:

■ **Were there big differences between your dreams and expectations? Why/why not?**

■ **Were there very different answers to the same questions from different group members? Why/why not?**

■ **Where do you think your dreams and expectations come from?**

TIME

(45 minutes for both parts)

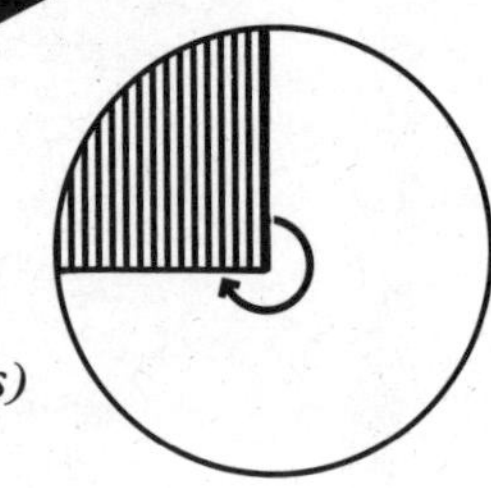

Part B

— Split participants into groups of 4. Ask each group to produce an annotated drawing of 'A Successful Person'. (Allow 15 minutes)

— Back in the big group, ask someone from each of the 4s to come forward in turn, stick up their poster and explain it to everyone.

— Discuss why people chose to depict 'Success' as they did.

Exercises two and three are designed as direct follow-ups to this one and should be done while it is still fresh in the minds of the group.

Second exercise:

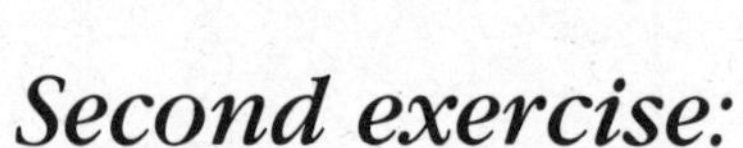

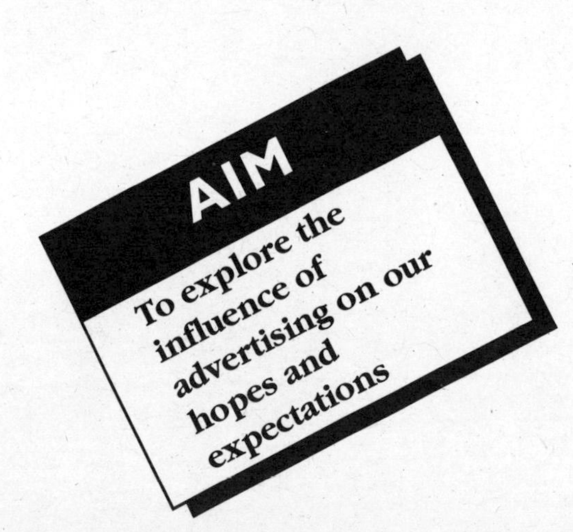

a series of adverts either cut out from magazines or videoed from TV (and the means to show them)

TIME

(25 minutes)

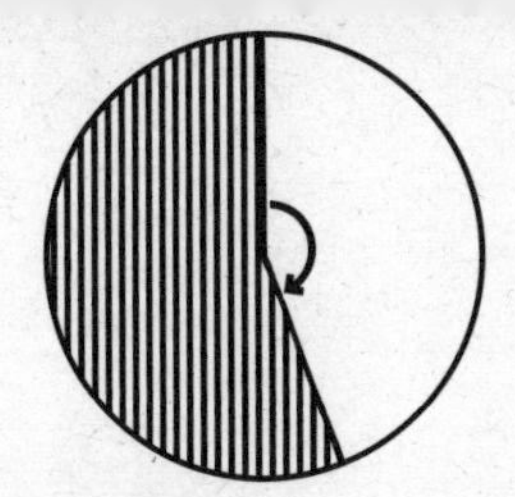

Part A : 'Reading' the adverts

— Show the group the adverts and discuss some or all of the following points:

- **What were your favourite ads and why?**
- **What kinds of people were held up as ideals in the ads?**
- **How were these ideal people used to sell the products?**
- **Which adverts were aimed specifically at young people? How did you know?**
- **How influenced do you think you are by adverts? Were any of your ideas of success in the first exercise formed by them? (People often claim that they are not influenced by adverts. Yet millions of pounds are spent on them every year. Is all this money, spent by highly sophisticated business people, wasted?)**
- **Charities like CAFOD, Christian Aid and SCIAF spend money on advertising. Is this money well spent?**
- **So is advertising a good or a bad thing?**

Part B: Making your own adverts

TIME

(50 minutes)

— Divide into groups of 6 or 7.

— Ask each group to prepare a TV advert for a new venture such as a Third World charity, a fund raising event, a magazine or newspaper. All members must perform in the finished ad.

— Tell them to decide:

- **the name of the new venture**
- **who they are hoping will 'buy' it**
- **what 'image' they want the product to have**

— After a set time (35 minutes) get the groups back together to act out their adverts.

— After each advert, ask the other groups to discuss what it was trying to achieve and how it tried to sell its product.

— Ask all the participants if they were ready to deceive in order to sell their products.

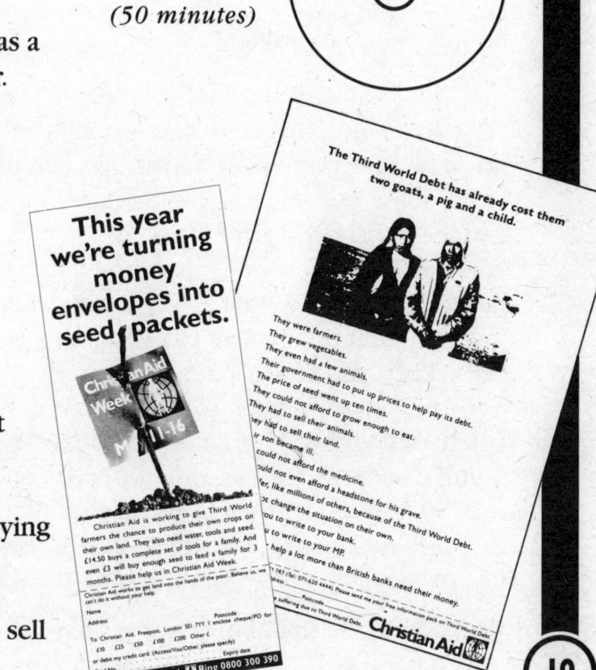

AIM

To help the group understand the very different lives of other young people in the world

TIME

(35 minutes)

Third exercise:

OTHER PEOPLE, OTHER LIVES

— Read some or all of the stories below with the group and discuss the questions which follow.

J. SOUTHWORTH/PHOTOFUSION

■ **Homeless young people on the streets of London**

Without a home

Tania is 17 and, like thousands of other young people, is currently living rough on the streets of London. This is her story:

"I was born in Glasgow. Dad left home when I was 10. My Mum was left to bring up me and my two younger brothers. She couldn't really cope. We started fighting badly when I was about 13 – and then, when I was 16, she made me leave school to get a job. All my money went to my Mum and, because she was working nights, I had to baby-sit for my brothers every evening. I hated the life and after one terrible fight I left home and came down to London to look for a job. I couldn't find one. I'm completely stuck. Without a job, I can't afford a place to live and if you haven't got a permanent address, you can't get a job.

"The only thing that keeps me going is my friends. What people don't understand is that life on the streets can be a good laugh sometimes. I know some people here can be horrible, but many others are friendly and they've looked after me well. The big problem though is money. You can get some by begging but I hate that – it's so humiliating. A lot of my friends make easy cash by smuggling drugs into night clubs, but if you do that the dealers pay you partly by giving you drugs. I know these keep you warm and take your mind off your problems but I'm not sure I want to get into them, even if everybody does and they laugh at me for not joining in. To be honest, though, I can see myself doing it soon. What else can I do? The only other way to make money is by prostitution. Some of my friends do that and say it's OK, but with AIDS and some of the weird people about, it's too scary for me.

"What will I be doing in 5 years? I haven't a clue. I'll probably still be here, I suppose."

Now Ask

- **What could Tania have done differently to have avoided ending up on the streets?**
- **What would you do now if you were her?**
- **What can be done about the problem of homelessness?**

In the City

Angel Muñoz is 18. He lives in a poor area of Santiago, the capital of Chile, with his mother, his brother, 2 sisters, his brother-in-law and his nephew. He tells his story:

CHRISTIAN AID/R. DUDLEY

■ Angel Muñoz, near his home Santiago, Chile

"At the moment, I'm at school. The rest of the class are 16. Let me explain why I'm two years behind everybody else.

"When I was younger, Chile was a dictatorship under General Pinochet and there were always soldiers on the streets. I remember once when I was passing a demonstration against him in the centre of town, some soldiers grabbed me. They made me take my shoes off and stamp out a fire that the demonstrators had lit.

SOUTH AMERICA

SANTIAGO

CHILE

"Many of my friends were arrested for being against the government. Some were killed by the military and their bodies were dumped in the river. I became very bitter and fell into bad ways, taking drugs and stealing to pay for them. When my best friend was arrested, I decided to rethink my life and spoke to a woman who runs a youth group in my area. It was the best thing I ever did. She encouraged me to go along to the group's meetings, where young people discuss their lives and what they want from them. I realised I didn't have to give up after all.

"So, now, I'm back in school studying as hard as I can. Also, with the rest of the group I work with the local children, trying to make them feel loved, so they don't make the mistakes I did. Though I'm much happier, I still feel angry and sick when I visit the rich areas of Santiago. I just don't understand how the people there can live like they do when so many of us are so poor. Anyway, the dictatorship is gone now (Pinochet lost the presidency in 1990) and I'm determined to have a proper future."

Now Ask

- **How have Angel's expectations changed in the course of his life?**
- **Why do you think getting involved in the youth group made such a difference?**
- **How has being involved in a group affected you?**
- **Do you think Angel is right to feel as he does in the rich areas?**
- **Have you ever had any of the same feelings that Angel has?**

NICK ROBINSON/PANOS PICTURES

■ Zambian women working in the fields to grow vegetables for their families

AFRICA

ZAMBIA

In the Country

Patience Ng'uni is 13 and lives in small village settlement in rural Zambia. She has been there since 1991, when her parents decided that they could no longer make ends meet in the town.

The area is very remote. There are no buses or health facilities; the nearest shops are 74 kilometres away. There is a primary school but no secondary one. When they moved, the family was given enough land to grow their own food by the government which wants to reduce the overcrowding in the towns.

Patience is responsible for grinding by hand the maize grown to make 'mealie meal'. This takes her several hours a day. She then makes the mealie meal into a thick porridge called 'nshima' by boiling it and constantly stirring so that it doesn't go lumpy. The nshima is eaten with vegetables or, occasionally, meat. Patience also helps her mother tend the plot of land where they grow vegetables like sweet potatoes and beans. The land is stony and dry, and Patience has to get the water in pots from a nearby stream. It's a lot of hard work.

And her hopes for the future? "To get married and start my own family, of course."

FOLLOW UP

Why not arrange a video showing of either 'Savithri' from Christian Aid or 'Big Lights, Big Cities' from CAFOD (see the Resources Section for details).

Now Ask

- **Do you think you would like to live like Patience?**
- **Many of the boys in Zambian villages head for the city when they are older. Though there are few jobs there and no social security, they see it as more exciting than rural life. What would you do if you were them?**
- **The city option is rarely open to girls, who are encouraged to stay at home by their mothers. What choices does Patience have?**
- **How would she draw a 'Successful Person' (as in Exercise 1), do you think?**
- **What difference has your education made to your life?**

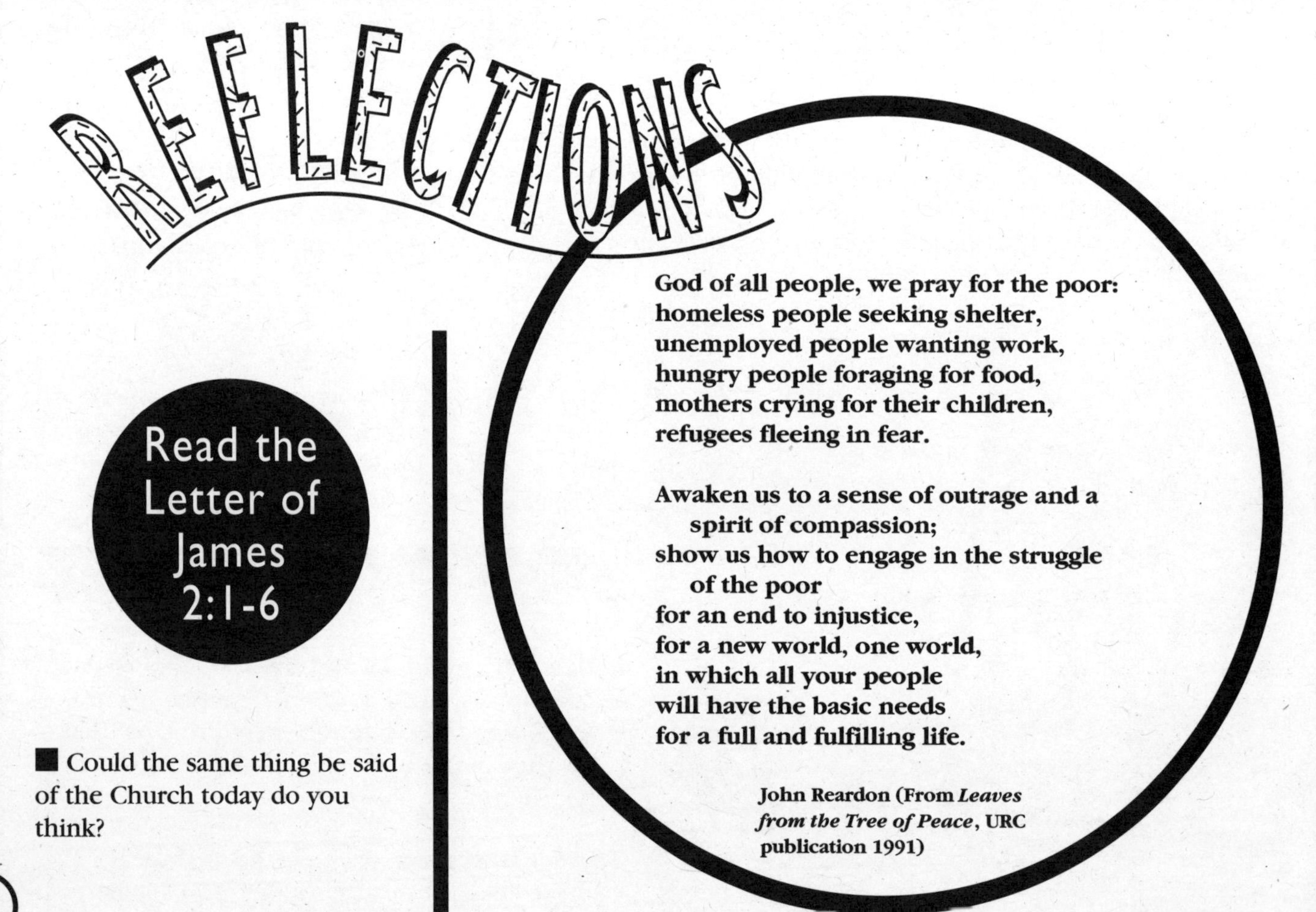

Read the Letter of James 2:1-6

- Could the same thing be said of the Church today do you think?

God of all people, we pray for the poor:
homeless people seeking shelter,
unemployed people wanting work,
hungry people foraging for food,
mothers crying for their children,
refugees fleeing in fear.

Awaken us to a sense of outrage and a
spirit of compassion;
show us how to engage in the struggle
of the poor
for an end to injustice,
for a new world, one world,
in which all your people
will have the basic needs
for a full and fulfilling life.

John Reardon (From *Leaves from the Tree of Peace*, URC publication 1991)

❹ How *IMAGE* conscious are you?

Part One:

Choose which of these two exercises you feel is best suited to your group. Whichever you choose, follow up with the discussion below and then go on to Part Two of the chapter.

Exercise A:
Making a tableau

TIME
(35 minutes)

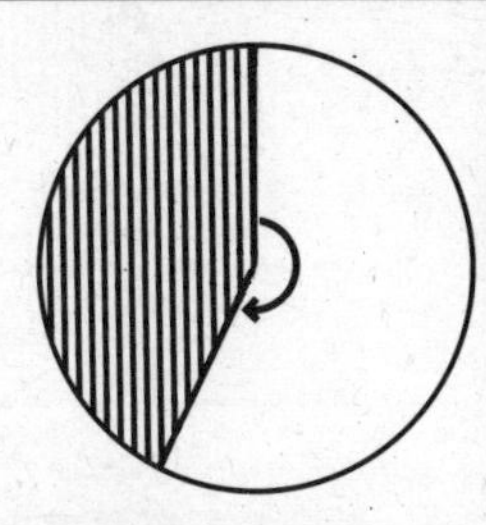

— Split the participants into groups of 5 or 6.

— Ask each small group to devise a tableau or stationary mime entitled 'The Third World'. Everyone in the group must have a role. (Allow 10 - 15 minutes.)

— Back in the big group, get each of the small groups to present its tableau in turn. After each one, see if the audience can explain what they saw.

— Move into the discussion.

flip-chart
marker pen

Exercise B:
Poster design

TIME
(40 minutes)

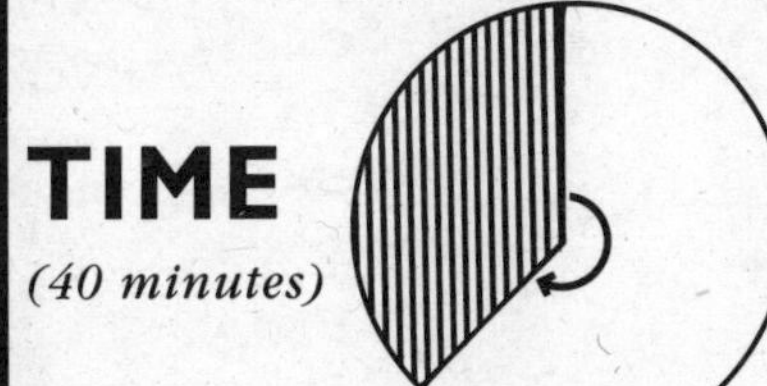

YOU WILL NEED

flip-chart
marker pen
a large sheet of paper
selection of felt-tips

— Split the group into 3s or 4s.

— Ask each small group to design a poster for CAFOD, Christian Aid or SCIAF depicting life in the Third World. (Allow 20 minutes.)

— Back in the big group ask one person from each group of designers to present and explain their poster.

— Display the posters and move into the discussion.

POINTS FOR DISCUSSION

— Ask the group to shout out all the words suggested by their posters or tableaux and write them on the flip chart. Then ask:

■ **Are the words mostly negative or positive?**

■ **Why do you think this is? Where do we get our ideas and images of the Third World from?**

■ **How would you feel about being described like this by people who live far away. Why?**

Part Two:

(30 minutes)

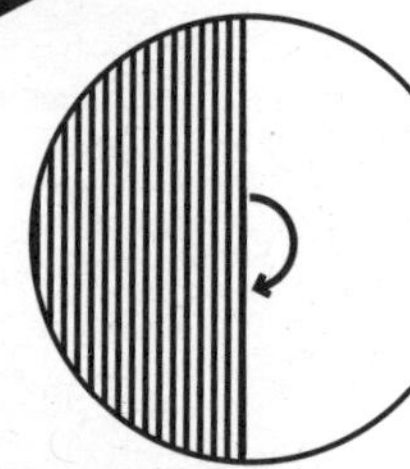

— Display the posters around the room.

— Invite the group to walk round and look at them carefully. Point out that all three organisations try to represent the Third World as the people in the pictures ask them to.

— Ask the group:

- **Are the images in the posters different from your images in Part One. Why/why not?**
- **Why do you think these agencies tend to show strong, positive images of the Third World in their posters and publications?**
- **If an organisation from India, for example, wanted to produce a poster depicting life in the UK, what would you like to be shown on it?**

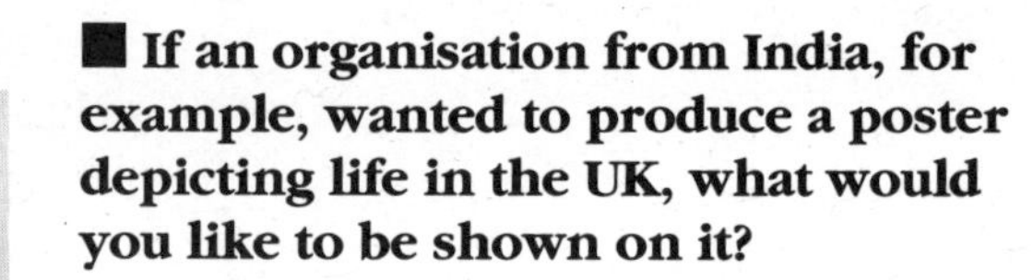

YOU WILL NEED

a variety of CAFOD, Christian Aid and SCIAF posters

Ask two people to read out the following:

CHRISTIAN AID/R. DUDLEY

Miriam is 18 and lives in a shanty town near Santiago in Chile. She says:

"I like living here. It is more honest. We know what life is really like. And there's more simplicity, solidarity and equality. I hate the fact that we have no decent education here, or health care, and that there's rubbish everywhere, but at least we work together to try and make things better. I'd rather be like this than be rich and have no idea how people really live."

CHRISTIAN AID/MAGGIE MURRAY

A few years ago, a teacher and some pupils from a wealthy part of an Indian city visited a local slum area. Veronica, who lived in the area, felt that the group, while well-meaning, had been so disgusted by the conditions there that they hadn't seen the people as real human beings at all. She wrote to the teacher the next day:

You want to help us! Good!
Yesterday you talked among yourselves and said: "We can have nutrition classes, saving schemes, classes on child care, etc."
Are these our needs? Our needs are more fundamental. We want understanding from you. Not contempt. Not annoyance. Not even pity... No charity please! Perhaps something else. Accept us as people!
Can you see us this way?
Yours sincerely,
Veronica.

POINTS FOR DISCUSSION

■ Clearly many people in the Third World feel misunderstood by western images of them. When in your own life have you felt misunderstood? What was it like?

■ Would you do the exercise in Part One any differently now?

FOLLOW UP

■ Show the video 'Africa: Our Own Story' from Christian Aid (see the Resources Section), which presents Africa through the eyes of Africans.

■ Ask the group, over the next few weeks, to look out for and collect stories about the Third World from the national media. Are such stories primarily positive or negative? Why is this? Compare them with the stories in *Christian Aid News, The CAFOD Magazine* or *SCIAF Review* – all available free from the respective organisations.

A PARABLE

There were 6 blind people. They heard that the king was visiting the next village, riding on an elephant. None of them had ever met an elephant and wondered what it was like. So they went to find out. Each of them went alone.

As the elephant stood there, the first held its trunk. The second a tusk. The third, an ear. The fourth, a leg. The fifth, its stomach. The sixth, its tail. Then they went home, all sure that they knew what an elephant looked like. They began to tell each other:

"Oh, it's fantastic," said the first, "so slow and soft, long and strong." "No," said the one who had felt the tusk, "it's quite short and hard." "You're both wrong actually," said the one who had felt the ear. "An elephant is flat and thin, like a big leaf." "No it isn't," said the fourth, who had felt the leg, "it's like a tree trunk." The other two joined in – "It's like a wall." "It's like a rope."

They argued and began to fight.

***Moral:* People often pretend that the little they know about something is the whole truth about it.**

***Justice:* To be always ready to admit that other people are quite different from what we thought.**

Simone Weil, French theologian (1909-1943)

For nearly 500 years the centre of gravity of African civilisation has been outside Africa. It is only by bringing it back to Africa that Africans can be said to have taken control of their destiny. Those from the outside act wisely only if we help them speed up the time when Africans once again will stand up and proclaim: "Our people are our mountains!"

James Oporia-Ekwaro, Uganda (1992)

5 *Food* glorious *Food*

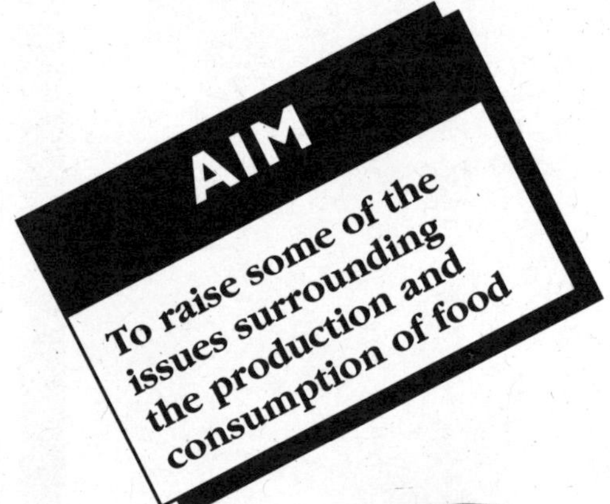

Part One:

THE FOOD QUIZ

YOU WILL NEED

paper and pens

— Depending on the size of the group, the following questions should be answered either in pairs or in 3s and 4s. Answers should be written down.

— You might like to warn the group that the quiz is not easy.

TIME

(30 minutes)

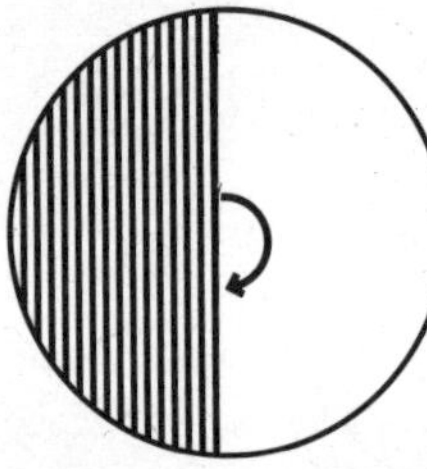

CHRISTIAN AID/S. CYTRYNOWICZ

■ **Elizabete, a Brazilian coffee picker, works to harvest the beans**

1 **What raw material brings in the most money on the planet, after oil? (Hint: it's edible.)**

2 **What do Pepsi Cola, Pizza Hut, Kentucky Fried Chicken, and Walkers crisps all have in common?**

3 **How many kilograms of grain are eaten by beef cattle to produce 1 kilo of meat?**

a) 0.5 kilo
b) 3 kilos
c) 7 kilos

4 **What percentage of the food needed to feed everybody on earth is produced every year? (To the nearest 10 per cent.)**

5 **How many children die every day from malnutrition?**

a) 400
b) 4,000
c) 40,000

6 **What percentage of food bought in the UK is thrown away?**

a) 10 per cent
b) 25 per cent
c) 50 per cent

7 **How many companies control over three quarters of the UK coffee market?**

8 **The World Heath Organisation recommends 2,600 calories a day for a healthy diet. To the nearest hundred, what is the average daily calorie intake in the UK and in Mozambique? (1 point for each.)**

9 **How much of the world's cultivable land is being farmed?**

a) 30 per cent
b) 50 per cent
c) 90 per cent

10 **How much out of every pound we spend on the most popular coffee brands goes to the workers in the Third World who grow and tend the crop?**

ANSWERS:
1) Coffee. 2) They are all owned by the same company (Pepsico). 3 c) 7 kilos. This is why 11 square metres of rainforest must be turned into grazing land to produce one beefburger. 4) 150 per cent - ie more than enough. 5 c) 40,000. 6 b) 25 per cent. 7) Two: Nestlé (Nescafé) and Philip Morris (Maxwell House, Kenco). Together they have a turnover greater than the Gross National Product (GNP) of every Third World country except Brazil, India and China. 8) UK - 3,252 (24th highest in the world); Mozambique - 1,632 (lowest in the world). 9 b) 50 per cent. 10) 8p (anything between 5p and 10p counts as correct).

— Read out the answers and ask people to mark their papers.

— Ask for the scores. (Any group that scored more than 5 did very well!)

■ Were there any answers which surprised you? Why?

■ Refer back to questions 2) and 7). What are the dangers of so much of our food being produced by so few companies? For the consumer here? For the people in the countries that produce the food?

■ Vegetarians sometimes use the answer to question 3) as a reason for not eating meat. Is it a good reason? Are there better ones?

■ Refer back to question 10). Tea and coffee workers are among the world's worst paid and treated. Think of some TV adverts for these products. How do they hide this reality? (See Chapter Six for information on fairly traded tea and coffee)

FOLLOW UP

1 *Supermarket search*

— Ask the group in pairs to go around their local supermarket with paper and pen, and to note down as many famous brand names as they can, the parent company and the product's country of origin. Ask them particularly to look out for supposedly rival products which are in fact owned by the same company.

■ **What was their most surprising discovery?**

CHRISTIAN AID/STUART FRANKLIN

■ **Workers picking pineapples on a Del Monte plantation in the Philippines**

2 *Think consumer power*

Encourage the group to buy food which has not been produced by the exploitation and suffering of people in the Third World. Ideas of how to do this are in Chapter Six.

Part Two:

SO WHY ARE PEOPLE HUNGRY?

YOU WILL NEED

paper and pens
'Why are so many people in the world hungry?' photocopied and given to each group
large sheet of paper to write answers on
marker pen

TIME
(35 minutes)

"Today we proclaim a bold objective: that within a decade no child will go to bed hungry, and that no family will fear for its next day's bread."

So said American politician Henry Kissinger after a World Food Conference in 1974. In fact, within a decade the Ethiopian famine was at its height. Now, the number of people who die from hunger every day is equivalent to more than 300 'jumbo jet' crashes – with no survivors. Why?

INSTRUCTIONS:

— Ask people to work in groups of 4 or 5.
— Each group must select from the list below, the statements which in their opinion are the three best and the three worst. (Allow 15-20 minutes.)

WHY ARE SO MANY PEOPLE IN THE THIRD WORLD HUNGRY?

1. **They are lazy.**
2. **The climate is too harsh.**
3. **Much of the best land in the Third World is used to grow food for the West.**
4. **There are too many wars. Money is used to buy weapons rather than food.**
5. **Their governments are corrupt and concerned mainly with lining their own pockets.**
6. **Western banks and big businesses make too much profit at the expense of the Third World.**
7. **People are badly educated.**
8. **The world is organised by the rich in such a way as to preserve their wealth.**
9. **They have become too reliant on charity.**
10. **They have too many children.**

— Get the groups back together and ask each one in turn for their answers and the reasons for them.

— Record the answers on the large sheet of paper. Use a tick for the best and a cross for the worst statements.

— See if there was any consensus and discuss why/why not. Does any answer have both a tick and a cross?

— Ask the small groups responsible to discuss why.

— Come back to this exercise after playing the game in Part Three and see if the groups' opinions have changed.

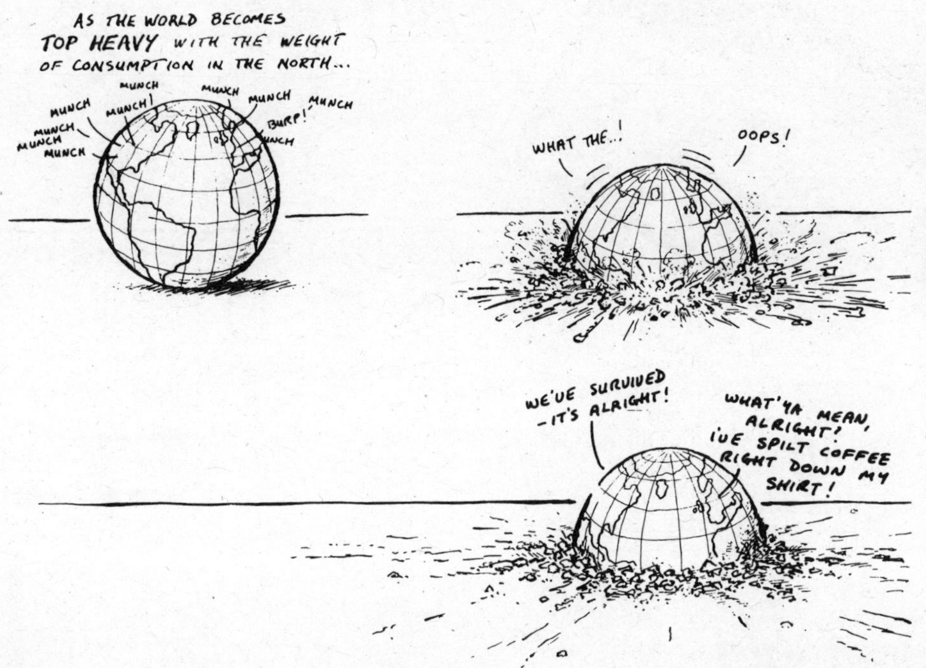

CHRIS MADDEN

CHRIS MADDEN

SOME POINTERS TO HELP THE DISCUSSION

Some answers are definite no-noes such as 1, 2, and 9. Others, such as 5, 7 and 10, are misleading and tend to put the blame on Third World countries themselves. The answers which have some truth are 3, 4, 6, and 8.

2 The Sahel has less than 35cm of rain a year (the UK receives about 110cm); 1 in 8 of all people in the world live in such desert areas.

3 Throughout the Ethiopian famine of the 1980s, it was possible to buy Ethiopian food in the UK. Meanwhile, millions of people are landless and so unable to grow food.

5 Some Third World governments, such as in Brazil, are controlled by wealthy groups who oppose policies aimed at enabling ordinary people to produce food for themselves. However, under the former President Nyerere, Tanzania was one of the few countries which tried to follow policies, despite many difficulties, which aimed to help the poor get more food. Since Nyerere's departure the government has been implementing IMF policies like everyone else.

8 Think of EC food mountains in times of famine.

10 By this statement people usually mean that the growing populations of poor countries are using up the world's resources and we will run out. But a child in the UK uses 30 times as much food and energy during its childhood as an Indian child.

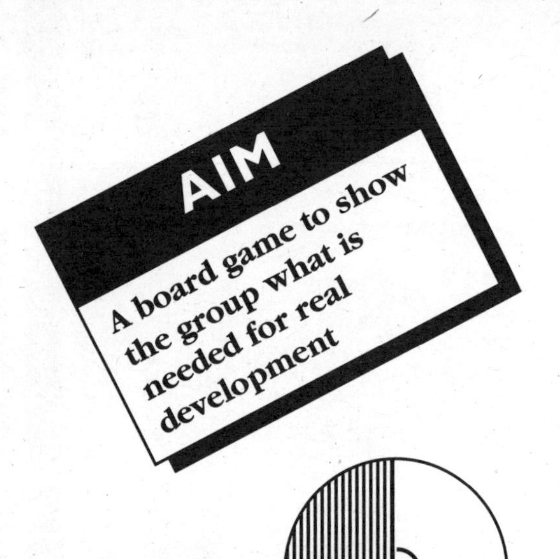

Part Three:

BREAKING THE CYCLE OF DISASTER

YOU WILL NEED

PER PERSON:
one set of the development cards (opposite)
one counter

PER GROUP OF 4:
one dice
one copy of the board (see pages 32-33)

TIME
(25-30 minutes)

INSTRUCTIONS

— Divide participants into groups of 4. Give each group 4 counters, a copy of the board, 4 sets of development cards and a dice.

— **Tell everyone:**

> "Each of you represents a farming village and your aim is to break the cycle of food shortages and lack of security which periodically results in famine and disaster by collecting the set of development cards which will help to improve your future."

— Read out the rules, then start the game.

RULES

1 Put all your counters on the start box. Place all the cards face up on the relevant space in the centre of the board. Take it in turns to throw the dice and move to the number shown.

2 As you move, pick up or return the development cards as shown. If you don't have a card to return when instructed to do so, miss a go.

3 Each player is allowed to hold only one of each card at any time.

4 When you have collected all 6, you have broken the cycle. If you have less than 6 cards, you continue with the game and enter another cycle.

— End the game when enough people have finished for the relevant points to have been raised. Then go to 'Points for Discussion'.

STEPHEN KING/CAFOD

CHRISTIAN AID/M. GOLDWATER

■ Eritrean farmers improve their fields

■ A farmer in Tigray ploughs his field

Development Cards

1 LAND SECURITY

When farmers know they have long-term use of their land, they no longer exploit it for short-term gain. Farmers need enough suitable land so they are not forced to overgraze, destroy trees or cultivate steep slopes which are easily eroded when it rains.

2 PEACE

Hope of a peaceful future enables farmers to make long-term plans and improvements.

3 WOMEN'S INVOLVEMENT

Women are responsible for much of the crop growing, fuelwood collection, food storage and food preparation. Only if women are involved in decision-making will development projects be relevant to the whole community.

4 COMMUNITY PARTICIPATION

A vital part of development. Activities like tree planting and livestock grazing control are only successful if the whole community joins in.

5 SUSTAINABLE AGRICULTURE

Peasant farmers know their environment but sometimes need support to maintain it. They need oxen, tools, access to cheap credit and fair prices for their produce. Technical advice on tree planting, erosion control, terracing and irrigation is also needed.

6 SUSTAINABLE POPULATION

Population growth rates tend to fall as countries develop. Women's education, child survival and security in old age all tend to result in people choosing to have fewer children.

Breaking the Famine Cycle Game

START HERE

POVERTY
Means no surplus food to store or money to spend on improved farming methods.

FAVOURABLE RAINS
Some surplus food grown.
MOVE ON 3

DEFORESTATION
Trees needed for firewood and building but overcutting leads to environmental crisis.
MISS A TURN

DROUGHT
Your reserve food exhausted.
THROW 6 OR GO T
'FOOD PRICES RISE'

Less than 6 development cards?
CONTINUE THE CYCLE

You have all six development cards ... WELL DONE! There are now real prospects for long-term development.

1 LAND SECURITY

2 PEA

4 COMMUNITY PARTICIPATION

5 SUS AGR

SOIL EROSION
Torrential rain washes your topsoil away.
RETURN ONE CARD

INAPPROPRIATE DEVELOPMENT
Project does not help poor farmers.
GO BACK 4 PLACES

PEACE
A just solution to the conflict agreed.
PICK UP ANY CARD. ALL PLAYERS PICK UP CARD 2

FAMINE
Families migrate in search of food.
RETURN ONE CARD

LAND REFORM
More land for small farmers boosts food production.
PICK UP ANY CARD. ALL PLAYERS PICK UP CARD 1

POOR FARMERS FORCED ONTO MARGINAL LAND
MISS A TURN

FAIR PRICES PAID FOR FARM PRODUCE
HAVE ANOTHER TU

INSTRUCTIONS

This game can be played by one or more people. You are a farming village(s) and your aim is to break the famine cycle by collecting the set of development cards. You need a dice plus a counter per player (coins will do). Place the counters on start, throw dice to move. Pick up and return development cards as directed, if you don't have a card to return miss a go. Each player is allowed to hold only one card of each number at any time.

ERRACES BUILT

ur fields are protected
m erosion. Crop yields
uble.

CK UP CARD 5

FOOD PRICES RISE

Livestock and land prices fall. Poor farmers must sell more and more to buy less.

MOVE TO 'DISEASE

DISEASE

Lack of food reduces your resistance to disease.

THROW 6 OR GO TO 'FAMINE'

FAMINE

Your hard-won development gains are lost.

RETURN 1 CARD

EMERGENCY RELIEF

Food aid needed in emergency but not a long-term solution.

MOVE ON 1

3 WOMEN'S INVOLVEMENT

TEMPORARY RECOVERY

Rain enables families to start farming again. Development agency provides tools and seeds.

ABLE
TURE

6 SUSTAINABLE POPULATION

TREE PLANTING PROGRAMME STARTED

ALL PLAYERS PICK UP CARD 5

WORLD RECESSION

.nterest repayments of your country's debt increase. No money left for development.

MISS A TURN

PRIMARY HEALTH CARE

Project improves the health of all the community.

PICK UP ANY CARD

AR

crops are destroyed.
y spent on arms, not
opment.

VE BACK TO FAMINE.
PLAYERS RETURN
RD NO 2

COMMUNITY MEETING TO PLAN DEVELOPMENT

ALL PLAYERS PICK UP CARD 4

WOMEN INCLUDED IN DECISION MAKING

PICK UP CARD 3 AND ANY OTHER. ADVANCE 1 PLACE

SUPERPOWER INTERVENTION

In your country.

THROW 6 OR ADVANCE TO 'WAR'

AFTER THE GAME

■ **What things helped you to break the cycle? What prevented you doing so?**

■ **How true to life do you think this is?**

■ **What part do we in the UK play in strengthening or breaking this cycle? How could we help Third World farmers more?**

■ How does Jesus say we will be judged here?

■ How can we do this more effectively?

How many more famines are needed before people in wealthy countries stop voting for politicians who only promise to maintain or raise the living standards of their electorate? Why can't they see that supermarkets stuffed with 35 different brands of chocolate bars and 22 assorted breakfast cereals are the reason why people in most countries don't know what a chocolate bar is, and don't eat a breakfast at all?

John Medcalf, *Letters from Nicaragua*. Published by Catholic Institute for International Relations (CIIR), 1988, London

There is no such thing as 'my' bread. All bread is 'ours' . . . and not only bread but all things for sustenance in this life are given on loan to us with others, and because of others, and for others, and through others for us.

Meister Eckhart, 13th century Christian mystic

If we Christians truly believed that we are all one Body,
the Body of the risen Christ, how many situations could we change!

That small mustard seed would crack open the hardest rock,
and we would level the Greed Mountains to lift up the valleys of misery.

Oh! If we could just live like real sisters and brothers!
Then the earth with all its treasures would become our Daily Bread,
and we would never more take the name of Our Father in vain.

Julia Esquival, a contemporary Christian from Guatemala

6 The TRADING Game

Quick starter exercise:

Ask the group to look at as many labels as possible (within the bounds of decency!) on the clothes they, or other group members, are wearing. Which countries do most come from? How many countries have supplied the group's clothes? Use this to introduce the theme of trade.

THE TRADING GAME

A large room with 7 tables (chairs optional)
50 A4 sheets of plain paper (same colour)
30 £100 notes (home-made or Monopoly)
2 sheets of coloured gummed paper
4 pairs of scissors
5 rulers
2 compasses for drawing circles
3 set squares (same size)
3 protractors (same size)
14 pencils
2 'Diagram of Shapes' charts (see p. 36)
6 A4 envelopes
6 country name cards (able to stand)
'Banker's Brief' and person to act as Banker

TIME
(90 minutes)

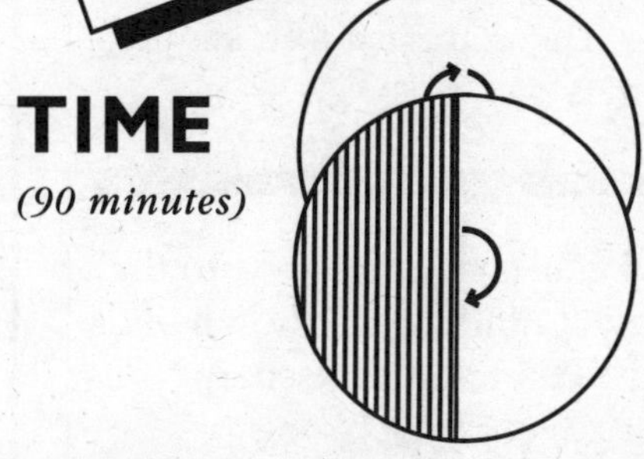

A simulation game for 15-30 people. (Ideal number: 30)

INSTRUCTIONS

1 PUT SETS OF EQUIPMENT INTO A4 ENVELOPES AS FOLLOWS:

2 sets of Grade A	2 sets of Grade B	**2 sets of Grade C**	**1 set for Banker**
2 scissors 2 rulers 1 compass 1 set square 1 protractor 1 sheet paper 6 £100 notes 4 pencils 1 country name card: (suggested) UK, USA or Japan	10 sheets paper 1 sheet gummed paper 2 £100 notes 1 country name card: (suggested) Brazil, India or Nigeria	4 sheets paper 2 £100 notes 2 pencils 1 country name card: (suggested) Ghana, Bangladesh or Tanzania	1 set square 1 protractor 1 ruler 1 pencil 'Banker's Brief' some paper

2 DISPLAY 'DIAGRAM OF SHAPES' CHARTS ONE AT EITHER END OF ROOM.

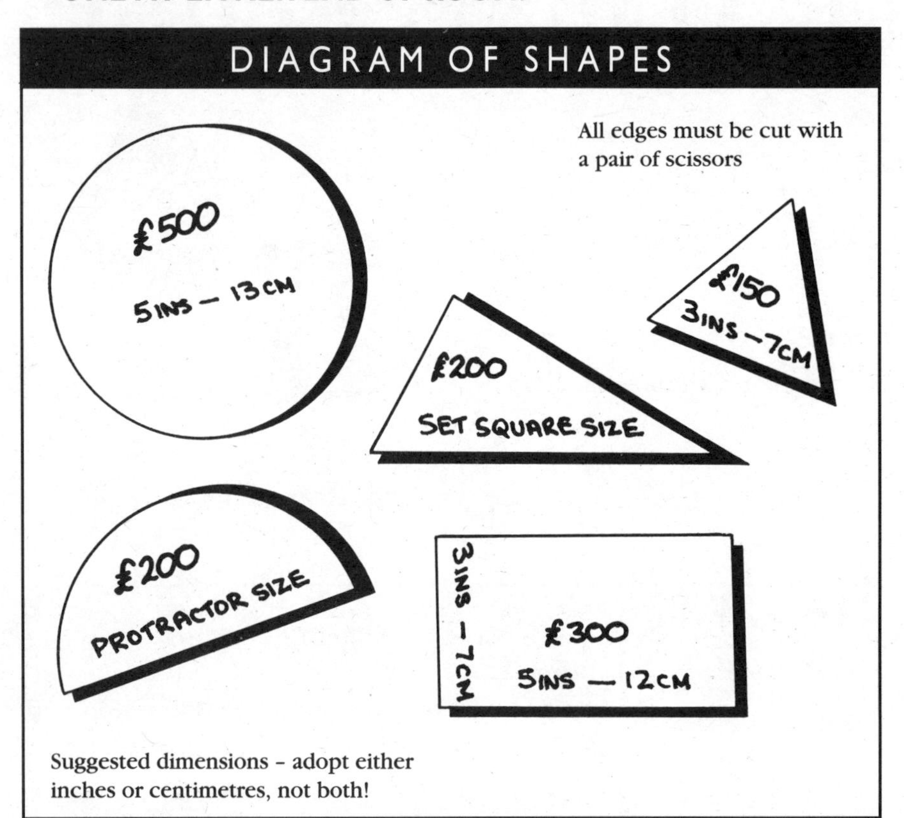

BANKER'S BRIEF

You will keep a record of the wealth made by the groups. Divide a sheet of paper into 6 columns, 1 for each country. When the groups bring you their shapes, credit their column with the appropriate amount. Do not accept sub-standard or ragged shapes. Measurements must be accurate.

Note: Keep spare paper and £100 notes yourself (and don't let them out of your sight once the game has begun!)

3 LEADING THE GAME

— Divide the group into 6 even-sized groups (except that Group A countries should have at least 4 people); assign each to a table. If numbers are small you can remove a Group B or C country and work with 5 groups.

— Give each group one of the envelopes.

— Ask any participants who have pencils or scissors about their person to surrender them to you.

CHRISTIAN AID/ELAINE DUIGENAN

■ **Burkina Faso: checking beans for export**

— Tell participants that they are now going to play a simulation game and, if necessary, what a simulation game is.

— Read out the objectives and rules of the game:

"Each group represents a country and your objective is to make as much wealth for your country as possible by using the materials provided. No other materials can be used. The wealth is made by manufacturing paper shapes. The shapes you can manufacture are shown on these charts (indicate 'Diagram of Shapes') and so is their value. The paper shapes are taken to the Banker in batches for checking and crediting to your bank account. You can manufacture as many shapes as you like – the more you make, the wealthier you will be."

— There are just four simple rules:

- The shapes must be to the exact dimensions shown on the chart and have sharp edges cut by scissors.
- You can only use the materials that have been given out.
- There is to be no physical force used during the game.
- The leader represents the United Nations and will intervene in any dispute.

— On the word 'GO' groups should open their envelopes, display their country name and begin.

— Say **'Go.'**

4 DURING THE GAME

— At the beginning of the game there will be much confusion and the group will bombard you with questions. Resist all temptation to answer these questions - just say "No further instructions", and then maintain tight-lipped silence. After a few minutes, participants should start moving around the room but let the initiative come from them, not you.

— Let manufacturing continue for 45 minutes, during which you should:

WATCH WHAT IS HAPPENING

Grade A groups will begin making shapes immediately, but will soon run out of raw materials (the paper) and probably try and buy some from other groups.

Watch how groups negotiate prices and determine 'terms of trade'. Note any alliances and deals, any cheating or stealing (don't intervene unless requested to), and jot down any interesting remarks you overhear. Feed all of this into the discussion at the end.

STIMULATE ACTIVITY

Once trading is under way, you can introduce new dimensions:

CHANGE MARKET VALUES

When the banker has a lot of one shape, announce that the market value of that shape has fallen. (Don't forget to make sure the Banker knows this.)

A parallel for this is the way some countries' economies are geared completely to the export of one product. When the market value drops the country concerned suffers badly. This happened in the 1980s with coffee in Uganda and elsewhere, for example. Also, rich countries can find that their technology has become outdated.

INCREASE THE SUPPLY OF RAW MATERIALS

Give one of the poorer groups an extra supply of paper and announce that a new deposit of raw materials has been found there. Notice the new interest the world begins to take in that country. (If the poor countries have formed an alliance, a sneaky trick is to give the new paper to one of the allies and see if they remain in solidarity – or go off with their new-found wealth.)

This parallels the find of oil or another important mineral, bringing about rapid change in the country concerned.

USING GUMMED PAPER

Two groups have gummed paper but don't know what it's for. Give a secret message to Grade As that any shapes with small squares of gummed paper attached will be worth 3 times as much. (NB: tell the Banker!) Don't tell them where to find the gummed paper though – let them find out for themselves.

This parallels when a country has a resource but doesn't realise how valuable it is - which happened all the time when Third World countries were colonised.

CHRISTIAN AID/ELAINE DUIGENAN

■ Alice Nambi, a Ugandan vegetable seller

■ Loading cotton bales for export, Nicaragua

PHILIP WOLMUTH

■ Loading bananas onto the Geest boat, Longhouse, Dominica

5 AT THE END OF THE MANUFACTURING TIME

Announce that the game has now ended and that the participants are no longer international traders. Ask the groups to go back to their tables and spend 5 minutes working out what happened to them in the course of the game. Ask them also to nominate a spokesperson willing to explain this to everybody. Bring all the groups together for debriefing.

PHILIP WOLMUTH

■ Roseau Market, Dominica

6 LEADING THE DEBRIEF

As in all simulation games, the debriefing is very important. Feelings can be running very high so try and keep it orderly and structured.

— Ask each spokesperson to describe what happened to their group during the game; give the other groups the right to respond.

— Ask what feelings the various groups had; discuss whether these have parallels in the real world. Was anybody surprised by the feelings they had?

— Ask the rich countries whether they shared their wealth. Why/why not? How did the poorer countries feel about this? Again, draw parallels with the world outside.

— Were any alliances formed in the course of the game? If so, did they work? Parallel their experiences with the EC or the various Third World cartels that have been tried over the years.

— Give your own impressions of what happened, including the remarks you overheard.

— Ask the Banker for his/her impressions, and the final score.

— Finish by asking the group how realistic they thought the game was.

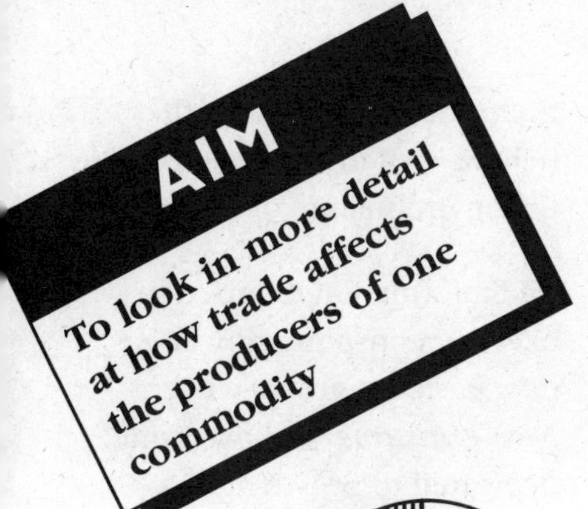

TIME

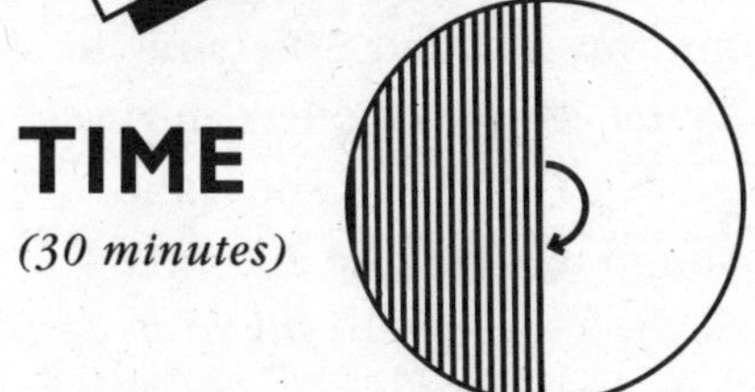

(30 minutes)

INSTRUCTIONS

— Divide into groups of 6 and give everybody in a group one of the following roles:

pickers and growers
packaging company
shipping company
importing company
wholesalers
retailers

— Make sure everybody understands their role in the process of supplying bananas to the UK.

— Give out paper and pens and give the pickers/growers a banana each. Tell everyone that the banana costs 10p in the shop.

PHILIP WOLMUTH

■ **Women packing bananas, Windward Islands**

Follow-up exercise:

SLICING THE BANANA

YOU WILL NEED

bananas (one for every 6 people in the group)
one large blank paper banana (as shown)
one large paper banana with real amounts filled in (as shown but keep concealed)
6 knives
paper and pens

— Put the blank banana on the wall, marked 10p. Ask each group to agree how much each member of the group will receive for their labour and other costs of the final banana price.

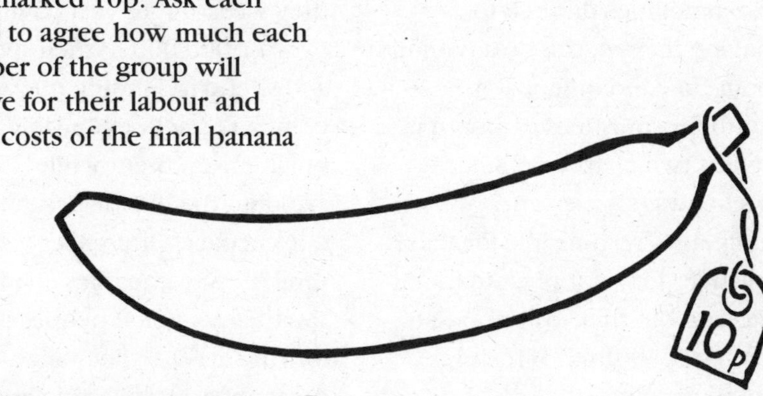

— After 5 minutes get each group to present its case.

— If the totals comes to over 10p, get the groups to negotiate between themselves until it comes to 10p.

— Reveal the actual situation.

To Retailer: 4p
To Importer/Wholesaler: 2p
Shipping Costs: 1p
Export and Handling Costs: ½p
Warehouse and Packaging Costs: 1½p
To Picker/Grower: 1p
10p

■ **How do the two sets of divisions compare?**

— Give the pickers/growers knives and allow them to share out the banana in the correct proportions. The pickers will be left with a tenth of each banana.

■ **How do the pickers feel?**

■ **Is the situation fair? If not, what can be done about it?**

This chapter provides an introduction to the basic trade situation; how power imbalances, together with human greed, ensure that the gap between rich and poor grows wider. If your group would like to explore in more detail how this works in the world, turn to the Resources Section for more things to do.

CONSUMER POWER

It is sometimes difficult to imagine that we can do anything about the kind of global economic injustices explored in the last two chapters. But, the good news is - we can! Companies responsible for these injustices may not react to moral pressure but they do respond to financial pressure. Which is where we come in.

Many young people in the UK, if they work for 40 years, will earn over £1,000,000 in their lives - and spend it! Finding out which companies act responsibly and buying from them while avoiding the 'baddies' can and does make a difference. Just think how companies changed their habits when people started 'buying green'. The biggest companies in the world are big only because we made them big, and we can threaten to make them small again unless they behave well towards people and the environment.

The information required to exercise consumer power is now easier to get than ever. *New Consumer* is a magazine dedicated to providing this information, and *Shopping for a Better World* is a quick and easy guide to socially responsible shopping. (See the Resource Section for how to get your copies).

Traidcraft sells fairly produced food of various kinds. Why not send for a catalogue? Think too about having a stall to sell its goods at the back of your church after the Sunday service - and allowing people to taste its tea and coffee. Serve fairly traded tea and coffee at your church events.

Finally, when you are shopping, look out for goods that are fairly traded.

The international trading system was devised by the rich to suit their needs; it ignores those of the poor.

Pope Paul VI (1963-1978)

We raise the wheat,
They give us the corn.
We sift the meal,
They give us the husk.
We peel the meat,
They give us the skin,
And that's the way they take us in.

Slave song, c 1855

Listen you who trample on the needy and try to suppress the poor, you who say: "When will the Sabbath be over, so that trading can begin?" Then you will again be at your tricks, the scant measure, the high price, the false weights. You who buy the poor for money and the needy for a pair of sandals. The Lord swears it by the pride of Jacob: "Never will I forget a single thing you have done."

Amos 8:4-6

7 *The War Game*

This chapter is about various kinds of conflict, from personal to international, each of which can be looked at in its own right. These are suggestions for making links between them, though these should not be strained, and may depend on the extent to which the young people have personal memory of a real war happening, which might be slight.

CHRISTIAN AID/S. FRANKLIN

■ **Soldiers in Davao City, the Philippines**

AIM

To help us understand how conflict starts – and continues

TIME

(35-55 minutes, allowing for rehearsal time)

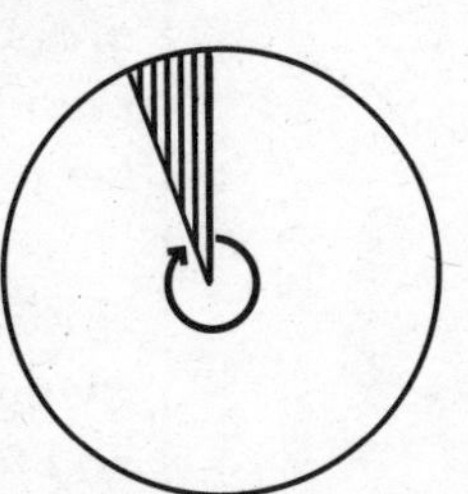

PART ONE – Our own attitudes to conflict

Exercise One:

WHAT HAPPENED NEXT?

photocopies of the story outlines below

STORY OUTLINES

■ **Jill and Clare**
On Saturday, Jill lent her college friend Clare a dress for a party. Clare had too much to drink at the party; in the morning she noticed a couple of cigarette burns in the dress. She bundles it up in a bag and gives it back to Jill on Monday morning at college, hoping Jill won't notice. But she does . . .

■ **Pete, Mary and Tracey**
Pete and Mary have been going out for a year. After Mary got back from a holiday with her parents, her friend Julie told her that Pete and Tracey went to the pictures together twice while she was away. Later that week Mary sees Pete and Tracey together in the park. She goes up to them . . .

■ **Jane and her parents**
Jane is 15. Her parents have let her go to a party on condition she is back by 11pm. She gets back at midnight, smelling of drink and tobacco. She tries to sneak in quietly, but her parents are waiting up . . .

INSTRUCTIONS

— Divide the group into 2s and 3s.

— Give each group one of the story outlines on previous page.

— Ask them to act out the situation and what happens next.

— Either ask them to improvise immediately or allow 15 minutes rehearsal.

— Repeat the exercise, BUT this time ask the groups to swap roles and try and act out peaceful resolutions to the situations.

— Ask the group:

■ **What have you learnt from the exercise about how conflict starts?**

■ **Does this teach you anything about the way wars begin?**

Excercise Two:

BEHAVING LIKE ANIMALS?

a large chart of 'The Animals'

INSTRUCTIONS

— Ask people to choose the animal they most resemble in times of conflict.

THE ANIMALS

OSTRICH
burying its head in the sand

DOVE
trying to make peace

RABBIT
running for cover

JACKAL
screaming and yelling into the night

LION
aggressively attacking

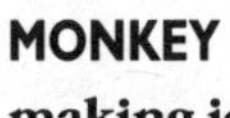

MONKEY
making jokes and creating diversions

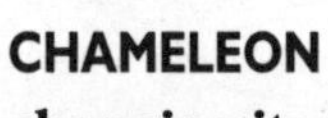

CHAMELEON
changing its story to fit in with whomever it's talking to

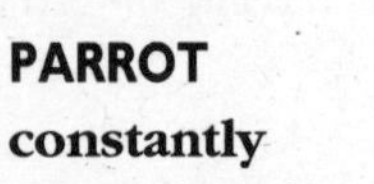

PARROT
constantly answering back

SNAKE
slyly making promises it has no intention of keeping

SEAGULL
flying into space and fantasising

SQUIRREL
storing up all the anger and hurt inside

TEDDY BEAR
being nice to everyone in the hope that they'll be nice back

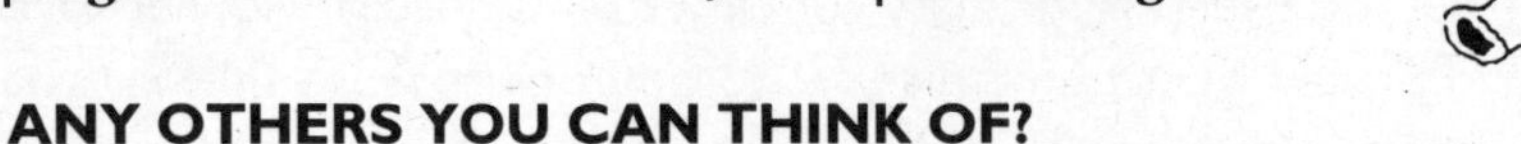

ANY OTHERS YOU CAN THINK OF?

— Ask everybody to act/walk/make noises like 'their' animal so that people with the same approach to conflict can find each other.

— Ask people with the same animal to share why they resemble it and, if there's enough trust, to give examples.

— Finally, ask everybody if there are any situations of conflict (real or imagined) in which they would be willing to use violence.

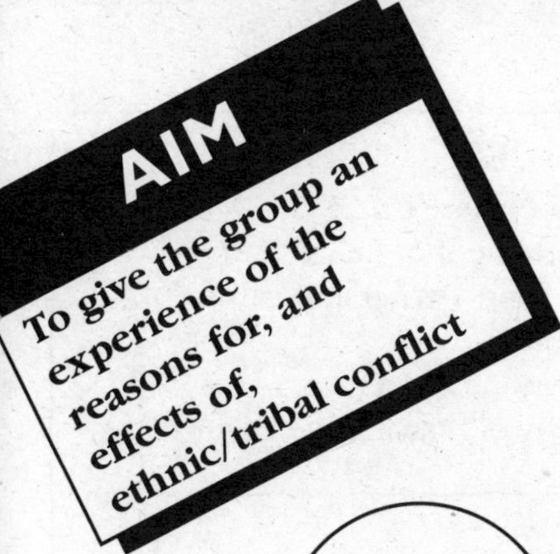

PART TWO

The Creed Island Game can be played by 8-24 people divided into 6 tribes. There should be at least 2 people per tribe so that discussion can take place. For small groups, the number of tribes can be reduced to 5 or 4 – in which case the Rantees and the Flumps should not be used.

TIME

(90 minutes including discussion)

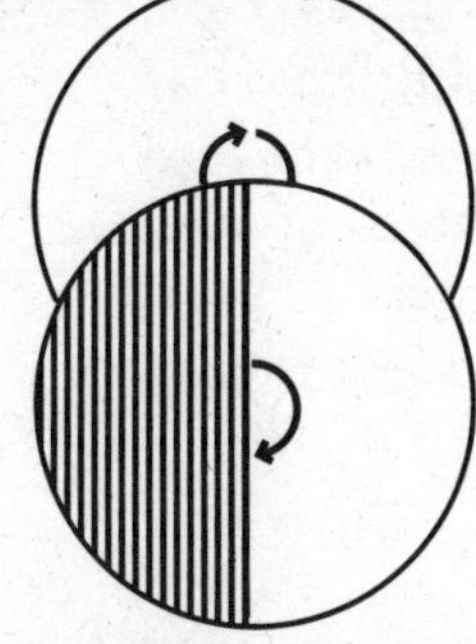

1 **The island outline drawn on card at least 20"x30" and divided into 43 squares numbered exactly as shown on the diagram. Include some mountains and outline a rectangle of 6 squares (2x3) more heavily than the rest.**

2 **'Rules of Play'and 'Tribal Rights' written up on posters.**

3 **Dice and shaker**

4 **Military Strike cards – 10 cards with explosions or bombs drawn on them which will be held by the Controller, along with some extra money tokens, a piece of paper and a pen.**

Continued overleaf

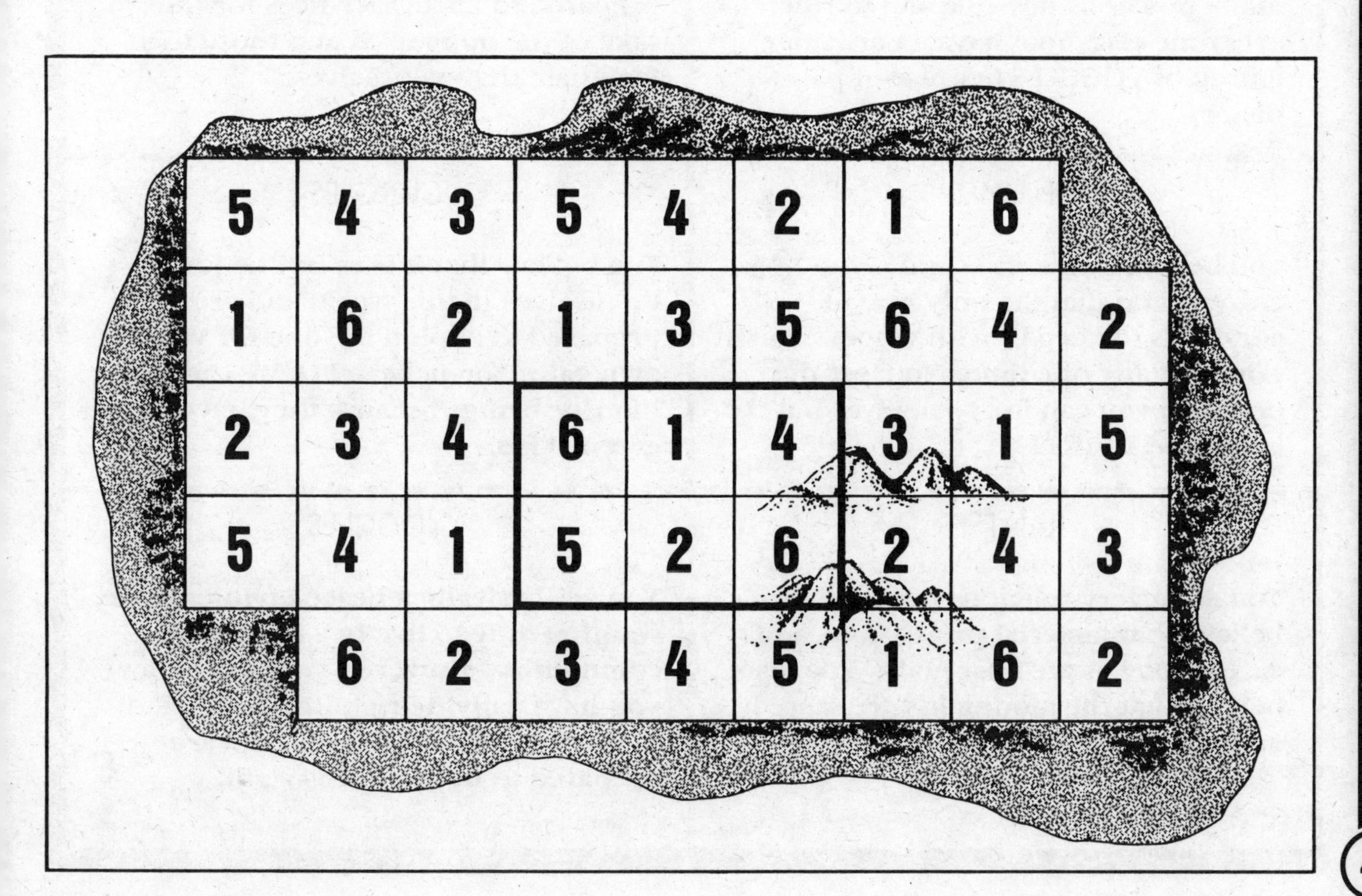

5 **Envelope for each tribe to include the following:**

YOGGLES
Tribe name card
'Statement of Belief'
43 Land Ownership cards (orange)
40 money tokens
Copy of 'Playing the Game'

BLERBS
Tribe name card
'Statement of Belief'
43 Land Ownership cards (green)
35 money tokens
Copy of 'Playing the Game'

RANTEES
Tribe name card
'Statement of Belief''
43 Land Ownership cards (red)
25 money tokens
Copy of 'Playing the Game'

GURGLES
Tribe name card
'Statement of Belief'
43 Land Ownership cards (blue)
30 money tokens
Copy of 'Playing the Game'

SNUBS
Tribe name card
'Statement of Belief'
43 Land Ownership cards (yellow)
35 money tokens
Copy of 'Playing the Game'

FLUMPS
Tribe name card
'Statement of Belief'
43 Land Ownership cards (pink)
20 money tokens
Copy of 'Playing the Game'

NB Land Ownership cards should be small cards about one quarter the size of the map squares. Each tribe should have a different colour (include the Creed Island map where appropriate)

STATEMENT OF BELIEF

SNUBS

You believe that you are superior to all other tribes; your ambition is to gain as much power as possible and to rule everyone else. You have a particular hatred of YOGGLES because of past history.

BLERBS

You believe in the equality of all peoples in the sight of God. You are prepared to make sacrifices for the sake of the oppressed and those less fortunate than yourselves.

FLUMPS

You believe you are second class citizens and that the only way to survive is to keep in with whoever is in power at any one time. You get the best deal you can for yourselves but try and avoid conflict.

GURGLES

You believe that it is everyone for themselves in this world and are prepared to exploit anyone for your own gain. You believe FLUMPS are inferior beings because they have green skins.

RANTEES

You are a very religious people who believe that material possessions and earthly power are false gods. You also believe that the mountains are sacred and want to live in them.

YOGGLES

You are basically a peace-loving people, wanting only to live in a close-knit community. However, you also believe you have a divine right to the block of 6 heavily outlined squares and are prepared to fight for this right.

RULES OF PLAY

1 Every player and tribe must play according to their 'Statement of Belief'.

2 These beliefs must never be made known to the other tribes during the course of the game.

3 No tribe or player can be excluded from the game except by military intervention.

4 At no time can any tribe have more than two consecutive turns.

5 Each tribe can do only 1 action each turn.

6 The ruling of the Controller on any matter cannot be questioned.

TRIBAL RIGHTS

Every tribe has the freedom to choose its own squares according to the throw of the dice.

Every tribe has an equal number of turns in strict rotation.

Every tribe is allowed up to 2 minutes in which to make its move.

INTRODUCING THE GAME

(15 minutes)

1 Split the group into 6 tribes and give each tribe their envelope.

2 Ask them to open the envelope, display their name card and read through their 'Statement of Belief'. (Make sure everyone understands these.)

3 Sit the tribes around the island.

4 Read and display the 'Rules of Play' which cannot be changed.

5 Read and display the 'Tribal Rights' which can be altered during the course of play.

6 Explain that the object of the game is for each tribe to establish and preserve itself consistent with its belief and ambitions.

7 Read through 'Playing the Game' before you start, to make sure everybody understands.

PLAYING THE GAME

STARTING THE GAME

The tribes throw the dice to see who starts. The dice throwing then moves in a clockwise direction.

LAND OWNERSHIP

Each time the dice is thrown, the tribe involved has to decide whether it wants a square of that number. If it does, it pays that number of money tokens to the Controller and places a Land Ownership card on the square. If the square is not wanted, play passes to the next tribe.

MILITARY STRIKES

Once a tribe has 3 ADJACENT SQUARES in a horizontal or vertical line, it can purchase a Military Strike card with 5 money tokens. The purchase is counted as a turn. If a tribe wants to attack a square, it places a Military Strike card there when its turn comes and throws the dice. The number on the dice is the number of people killed in the tribe attacked. Each tribe is 10 times the number of actual players. (eg: 3 players = tribe of 30) The Controller keeps a record of tribal numbers as the game proceeds. If the attacking tribe has a larger population than the one attacked after the dice has been thrown, then it takes the square. Each Military Strike card can only be used once and is then returned to the Controller. If a tribe's population falls to zero, it is out.

CHANGING TRIBAL RIGHTS

If a tribe obtains 6 squares together in a vertical or horizontal RECTANGLE formation, it has the political power to alter or add to the list of 'Tribal Rights' – though nothing that contradicts the 'Rules of Play'. The alteration counts as one turn. The tribe can, however, make further changes so long as they retain the rectangle. If a tribe loses political power any changes to rights it has made stay in place until changed by another tribe.

DIGGING FOR GOLD

A tribe can obtain more money by announcing that it is 'Digging for Gold' before throwing the dice. If a 3 or 6 is then thrown, the Controller gives that number of money tokens to the tribe.

Continued over page

OTHER COURSES OF ACTION

As play proceeds, any tribe can decide not to throw the dice but take a different COURSE OF ACTION. For example:

a) To bargain for the purchase of a particular square owned by another tribe
b) To sacrifice its turn in order to assist another tribe by giving it money, land or military support
c) To try and make a pact with another tribe to work together or share power

All such proposed moves must be referred to the Controller for approval first and must be completed within 2 minutes.

NOTE TO CONTROLLER

Creed Island is an open-ended game in which the players determine the outcome. It is impossible to anticipate everything that might happen. You must allow or disallow actions as fairly and consistently as you can. If an action has a parallel in reality, it should be allowed; if it would be impossible in reality, it should not.

If the game needs additional stimulation at any point, you can play 'God' by announcing natural disasters that may affect some tribes, eg a tidal wave which wipes out several squares.

There may not be a clear end to the game or any obvious winner. You should stop play when you feel the points have been made or nothing new is likely to happen. There should be at least 45 minutes play.

The game is likely to produce strong emotions. Don't worry about this - simply feed them in to the post-play discussion.

AFTER THE GAME

Each game played will produce a different situation and reactions. Try and tailor the discussion to whatever has just happened and encourage the groups to make real-life parallels with this.

- Ask each tribe to read out its 'Statement of Belief'. Do the other tribes think this was lived up to?
- What feelings did each of the tribes have as the game progressed?
- In what ways were tribal rights changed and for whose benefit?
- Did the game bear any resemblance to real life? In what ways? Try and think of specific parallels.
- How were wealth and political power used? Was this realistic?
- What would have happened if there had been no Military Strike cards?

(Creed Island Game devised by Bernard Grimsey, 64, Long Lane, Aughton, Ormskirk, L39 5BT. Tel: 0695 423849)

- How many causes of war can the group think of? Try to give examples of wars with these causes from history or the present.
- Where do you know of where there are ethnic/tribal wars, as in the game? Why do you think these happen?
- Is war ever justified? Should Christians ever fight in wars?
- What has war to do with poverty and development?

HINTS FOR THE LEADER

A war is defined as any conflict in which more than 1,000 people have died. War is one of the main causes of poverty and one of the biggest barriers to development. It destroys crops and land, disrupts market centres and transport links, and forces people to flee. Money that could be spent on improving the lives of the poor goes on weapons - which puts countries in debt and discourages foreign investment. Military research involves scientists who could otherwise be employed in socially useful research.

Ask the group to look out for reports of wars in the newspapers and on the television. These can be reported back at the next meeting.

PART THREE - The Arms Trade

for older young people

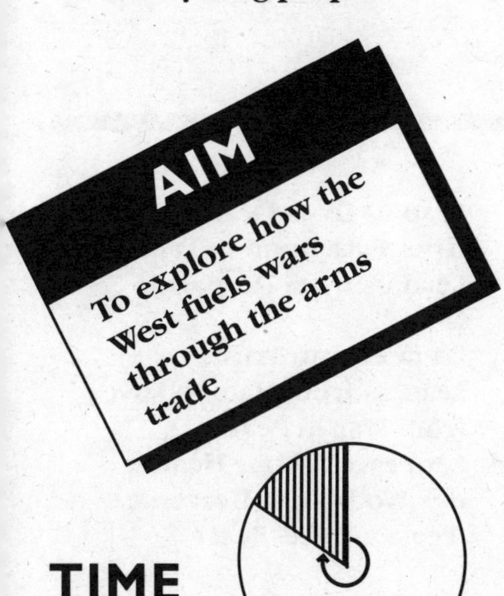

TIME

(50 minutes)

YOU WILL NEED

video 'Deals in Destruction' from CAAT (see Resources Section) and the means to play it

— Show the video. (30 minutes)

— Ask for reactions.

■ What did people find particularly surprising? Horrifying? What made them most angry?

■ Do UK job losses in the defence industry give you a different perspective on the arms trade?

The shelf-life of this book is likely to coincide with a period of enormous and rapid change in the world of international arms trading. The best way to keep in touch with the latest developments and find out what young people can do is by consulting Campaign Against the Arms Trade (see Addresses Section).

WAR FACTS

■ Of over 136 wars between 1945 and 1992, in which over 22 million people died, all but 3 were in the Third World.

■ There have been over 4 times as many war deaths in the 20th century as in the previous four centuries combined.

■ 56 per cent of western arms sales to the Third World in the 1980s went to countries with 'highly repressive governments'.

■ The world's rich countries devote over $500 billion a year to military spending, but just $47 billion to aid the development of the poorer countries.

■ UK military operating costs for 2 days of the 1991 Gulf War were £7.2 million - the same as the entire government budget for African famine relief in the same year.

■ Six times as much money is spent every year on weapons research as on health research.

(Figures from Stockholm International Peace Research Institute, 1992)

The following quotations are all from the 1991 Gulf War:

"The Saddam Hussein regime is now clearly heading for early destruction. We can thank God for that."

Daily Mail

"Jihad against Saddam, the enemy of God is one of the greatest forms of holy war for the sake of God."

Sheik Abdul-Aziz Bin Baz, Saudi Arabia's leading interpreter of Islamic jurisprudence

"Every time the sirens sound, we rush to this mountain to shout Allah Akbar (God is great) and pray the missiles find their targets in Tel Aviv."

Young Palestinian, West Bank

MIKE NELSON/AFP

"The Jewish God will not allow this murderer Hussein to succeed. God will defend the State of Israel."

Phone-in caller, London

"If Mr Bush makes the mistake of attacking us, he will repent it for ever. If he depends on technical facilities, we are depending on God."

Saddam Hussein, President of Iraq

"Matthew reminds us that the meek shall inherit the earth."

George Bush, President of the USA

- **How do you feel seeing so many different people all convinced that God was on their side?**
- **Whose side was God on?**

Wherever the strong exploit the weak; wherever the rich take advantage of the poor . . . there the work of making peace is undone.

Pope John Paul II, Coventry 1982

Lead us from Death to Life
from Falsehood to Truth;
Lead us from Despair to Hope
from Fear to Trust;
Lead us from Hate to Love
from War to Peace.
Let Peace fill our Hearts,
our World, our Universe.
Peace Peace Peace

Multifaith prayer of peace, said at noon all over the world, every day

O God!
Make good that which is
between us,
unite our hearts
and guide us to paths of
peace.

Muslim prayer

Peace I leave with you,
my own peace I give you,
a peace the world cannot
give, this is my gift to you.
Do not let your hearts be
troubled or afraid.

John 14:27

8 On the *Move!*

Starter exercise:

WHAT ARE REFUGEES?

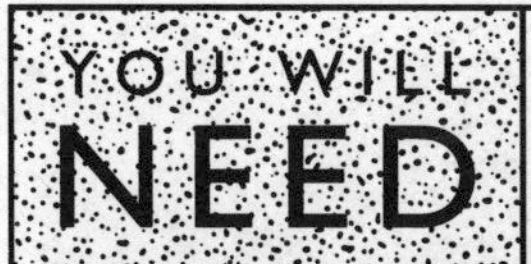

paper and pens
'Refugee Glossary' written up on large paper

TIME
(20 minutes)

— Split the group into pairs. Give each pair a piece of paper and a pen.

— Ask each pair to write down what they understand by 'refugee'.

— Ask them to read out their definitions.

— Reveal the official definition by sticking up the 'Refugee Glossary'; see who got closest to it. Make sure everyone understands all the terms.

● **REFUGEE**
The United Nations definition is 'a person who has left their own country owing to a well-founded fear of being persecuted for reasons of race, religion, nationality, membership of a particular social group or political opinion.' It is up to the government of the new country to decide if someone applying for refugee status fits this definition.

● **ASYLUM SEEKER**
Someone who has fled his or her country and is seeking refugee status.

● **INTERNALLY DISPLACED PERSON**
Someone who has left his or her home in fear of persecution, but has not crossed an international border.

● **IMMIGRANT**
One who migrates to a country with the intention of settling there.

Read out the following and ask the pairs to write down if they are true or false.

1. **One third of all immigrants settling in the UK every year are refugees.**
2. **Most of the world's refugees flee to rich European countries.**
3. **The UK has one of the lowest proportions of refugees in its population of any country in the world.**
4. **More people emigrate from the UK every year than come in as immigrants.**
5. **Over the past 10 years, 300 people a day have had to leave their homes somewhere in the world through fear of persecution.**
6. **Thirty per cent of people who seek asylum in western Europe are rejected.**
7. **Over 100,000 people arrive in the UK every year as asylum seekers.**
8. **The number of official refugees in the world is currently the highest ever.**

(Answers page 50)

ANSWERS

1 *False. The true figure is less than 10 per cent.*

2 *False. Only 5 per cent of the world's refugees live in Europe; around 83 per cent live in poor countries.*

3 *True. One person in 569 in the UK is a refugee - as opposed to 1 in 314 in France and 1 in 4 in Jordan.*

4 *True.*

5 *False. It's 3,000 a day.*

6 *False. 45 per cent are rejected.*

7 *False. It's 13,000.*

8 *True. There are now over 15 million refugees in the world. During and after World War Two there were over 60 million 'refugees' in Europe, without official status.*

— Ask people how they got on. Which answers did people find most surprising?

CHRISTIAN AID/S. FRANKLIN

■ **Refugees from Tigray in the Wad Kowli camp, eastern Sudan.**

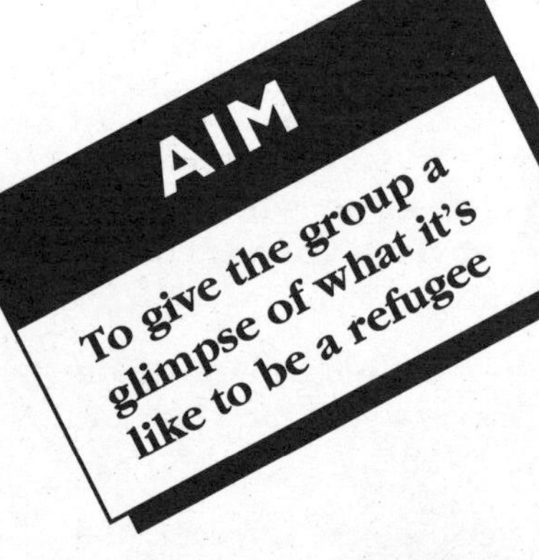

TIME

(30 minutes)

Main exercise:

LEAVING HOME

INSTRUCTIONS

This is an exercise in visualisation. People need to be relaxed and silent - so take some time to establish this. Take the exercise slowly. Gentle music in the background may help.

Tell the group that they are going to do an exercise which needs them to use their imaginations as much as possible. Ask them to get into a comfortable position, to close their eyes and to consciously relax their bodies . . . legs . . . arms . . . faces . . . chests . . . Ask them to listen to the sound of their own breathing. When people are relaxed, read out the following, adding things in your own words if you wish, and leaving pauses where the dots are:

You are living in a small village in a remote part of Africa . . . Take some time to visualise the village . . . What can you see . . . hear . . . smell . . . ? At the moment you are in your house but you know you are about to become a refugee and do not have long to prepare for a journey into the unknown. The army is getting close, you have heard about massacres in nearby villages and decide to flee . . . You can even hear gunfire in the distance

CHRISTIAN AID/IAN BERRY

now . . . You are to leave on foot and hope to find someone in a town 30 miles away who has a truck which can take you to the coast where you might be able to find a boat to take you to a safe place . . . The only certain thing is that you will probably never return to the place you are now. Look around your home for the last time . . . What is it like . . . ? Visualise it as carefully as you can . . . the rooms . . . the furniture . . . What will you most miss about your home . . . ?

Nonetheless you know there is no time to become too sad . . . you must pack for the journey. You have only a few minutes to pack . . . What are you going to take . . . ? What will you need . . . ? They must all be things you can actually carry. Take some time to decide . . . (Allow a few minutes.)

So now you are packed and must begin the long walk . . . What are your feelings as you leave and look back at the village? How many people are travelling with you . . . ? Are all your family with you . . . ? What is the mood among the new refugees . . . ? Do people talk or are they silent . . . ? What is the weather like as you set off . . . ? How long do you walk for that first day . .

Where do you spend the first night . . . ? Have you brought what you need?

How long does it take to get to the town . . . ? Is everyone still with you. . . ? What were the worst parts of the journey . . . ? How is the mood now . . . ?

When you get to the town, you manage to find a truck driver who will take you to the coast, but he demands as payment the most valuable possession you have with you. What is this? How do you feel as you hand it over . . .?

(continued overleaf)

JEREMY HARTLEY/OXFAM

Aid for flood victims, Sudan, 1988

CHRISTIAN AID/PAUL O'DRISCOLL

Mozambican refugees rest after crossing into Zimbabwe

STUART FRANKLIN/MAGNUM

Refugees pass through Wad Kowli, near Gedaref, Sudan

And so you board the truck. It's very crowded with everybody on board and very bumpy. Going round a bend, some of the bags fall off. You all shout but the driver doesn't hear . . . The bags are left far behind. . . Were any of the bags yours . . . ? How do you feel . . . ? Are you willing to share some of your possessions . . . ?

Now, you hear funny noises from the truck's engine . . . Sure enough, it breaks down . . . You all get off but are now too tired to carry all your luggage. You must reduce its weight considerably. What do you leave behind . . . ?

The walking begins again and lasts 2 days. What are those days like . . . ? Does anyone give up . . . ?

Finally, you reach the coast and a port . . . After much haggling a captain lets you board his boat, but again demands your most valuable possession. What is this . . . ? How do you feel as you give it to him . . . ? How do you feel as you board the ship . . . ? What are your quarters like. . . ?

Before you sail, the captain says that his vessel is overloaded. You must all leave a heavy item behind . . . Finally, you set sail for your new home, wherever it might be . . .

– End the exercise here by saying:

"The exercise is over. So when you're ready, but only when you're ready, return to this room. Don't hurry back and when you are back don't move, just open your eyes. I'll let you know when everybody's back."

CHRISTIAN AID/IAN BERRY

■ Ethiopian refugees walk up to Melecle, a food distribution centre, during the 1987 famine.

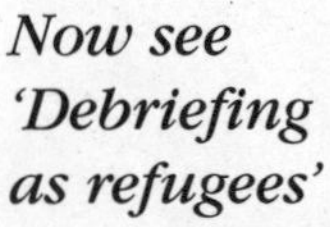

Now see 'Debriefing as refugees'

(This visualisation is based on 'A refugee simulation' from *Simulation Games 3* by Pat Baker. © The Joint Board of Christian Education, 2nd Floor, 10 Queen's Street, Melbourne 3000, Australia)

DEBRIEFING AS REFUGEES

— Give people time to collect their thoughts. Then ask them to share their experiences in pairs or small groups.

■ What were your home and village like? How did you feel as you left them?

■ What did you take with you? What were the most popular items? Were there any that only one person took?

■ As the story unfolded, did you feel you had taken the right things? Did you take blankets? What did you eat?

■ What was the walking like?

■ What were your feelings as the journey progressed?

■ What were the worst times?

■ How did you feel when you had to give up your possessions?

■ How did you feel as the ship left the port?

POINTS FOR DISCUSSION

■ What did you learn about refugees from the exercise?

■ How do you think refugees feel when they get to their new country?

■ Have there ever been times when you've felt an outsider in a situation? What was it like?

■ What can be done to make newly arrived refugees feel more at home?

TWO CASE STUDIES

FROM TIGRAY TO SUDAN

1

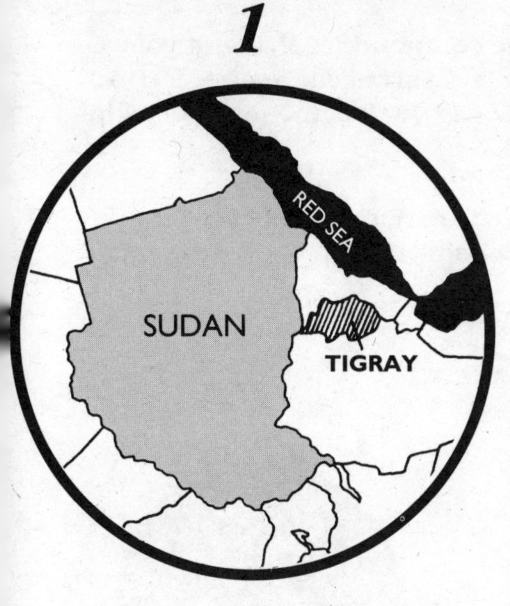

Berhane Araya is 18. He is a Tigrayan refugee living in the Um-Rakuba (meaning 'home') refugee camp on the eastern Sudanese border. The camp is run by the Sudan Council of Churches.

Berhane works as a tea-maker in a café in the camp (which is quite village-like) where he earns 200 Sudanese pounds a month. But the charcoal needed by a family for fuel costs 200 pounds a sack and lasts a week. Still, Berhane is lucky to have any income at all. Most of the men are unemployed and sit around his café all day. Only the people who arrived in the camp soon after it opened (15 years ago) have any land to grow food. The rest of the refugees rely on food relief, supplied by various charities.

Berhane wants to go home to Tigray, but he listens to the radio every day and hears that even though the war is now over the political situation is still not settled. He is likely to be in the camp for many years yet.

■ **Ask the group to put themselves in Berhane's position. How would they feel? What would they do?**

FROM ERITREA TO LONDON

2

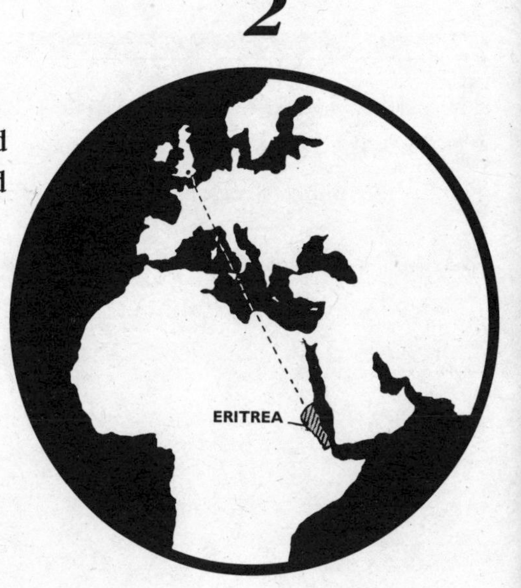

An Eritrean refugee living in London, who wanted to remain unnamed, said in 1990:

"My father, who was strongly opposed to the Ethiopian government which occupied our country at the time, was killed by their security forces in 1975. My younger sister was tortured to death in prison. She was charged with opposing the government. The youngest member of our family was killed when Ethiopian planes bombed our village in 1980. Nobody knows where the bodies of my family are laid. The only crime of my family was to say no to injustice.

"For many years I have had chronic insomnia and I lie awake tormented by painful memories. When I do manage to fall asleep I dream of violence, killing, tortures and screams."

(From *We Left Because We Had To*, published by The Refugee Council.)

■ **The war in Eritrea has since ended. This refugee has not gone home. Why do you think this is?**

1 **If the group wants to learn more about refugees, contact the Refugee Council or the Office of the United Nations High Commissioner for Refugees (see Addresses Section at the back).**

2 **Find out about any refugee communities living in your area. Are they being helped to feel part of society here? Do they have community associations which could provide people to come and talk to your group?**

3 **Write to CAFOD for a list of the materials and video produced to support its refugee campaign.**

Read Psalm 137

Psalm 137 depicts the emotions of a people in exile. In 586 BC King Nebuchadnezzar of Babylon, with the help of the Edomites, captured Jerusalem and burned the great Temple of Solomon. This was a devastating blow to the Jews, for whom the temple was a central expression of God's presence among his people. They were then shipped off to Babylon – exiled from Zion, the land they loved. It was a time of great crisis. How could God have allowed this? Could their faith survive in a foreign country?

- **What are the different emotions described? Are you surprised by any of these?**
- **Which of the emotions do you think are felt by refugees today?**

There is no sorrow above the loss of a native land.

Euripides (Greek dramatist, 5th century BC)

Everyone is quick to blame the foreigner.

Aeschylus (Another Greek dramatist, 5th century BC)

9 Rights and Wrongs

Starter exercise:

Ask the group to think about their own rights. What are they legally allowed or not allowed to do below the age of 16? At 16? At 18? How are these rights decided? Are they sensible? Fair? Use this discussion to introduce the broader issue of human rights.

'THE RIGHTS ORDER'

1 envelope for each group of 3 or 4 containing the 11 numbered situations below, written out on strips of paper

SITUATIONS

1 **Unemployment** – jobs are very difficult to find; there is high unemployment.

2 **Voting** – there are no proper elections and the government is a self-appointed dictatorship.

3 **Poor Health Care** – there are a general lack of medical facilities and health workers.

4 **No Religious Freedom** – certain religions are not allowed to practice their faiths. If they do, believers are persecuted.

5 **Poor Housing** – there is little chance of getting somewhere decent to live.

6 **No Unions** – trade unions and strikes are banned despite bad working conditions.

7 **Few Educational Opportunities** – it is very difficult for people to get a secondary education unless they are rich.

8 **Torture** – torture is practised against 'enemies of the state'.

9 **No Free Speech** – people who speak out against the government are imprisoned.

10 **Racism** – people are discriminated against on grounds of race.

11 **Travel Bans** – people are not allowed to leave the country.

CHRISTIAN AID/JENNY MATTHEWS

■ Mothers in El Salvador protesting against the disappearance of their children

■ A street protest, in Salvador, Brazil

CHRISTIAN AID/E. BERRIOS

INSTRUCTIONS

— Divide the group into 3s or 4s.

— Distribute the envelopes.

— Tell the groups that the envelopes contain examples of situations where people suffer oppression.

— Ask each group to rank the situations according to how serious they think each is, most serious at the top. (Allow 15 minutes)

— Meet back in the big group to discuss the results.

■ **Compare the rankings of the different groups? Were they similar? Why/why not?**

Ask any two groups which chose very differently to argue their cases.

■ **Do any of the situations describe life in the UK? How high up did the groups place these in their rankings?**

■ **What other things would you consider to be human rights? Tick off those mentioned which are on the official United Nations list of human rights (page 57); read out the rest of the list.**

■ **Is there anything not on the UN list that should be? Anything that is, that shouldn't?**

■ **Are there any things human beings need which cannot be described as rights?**

HUMAN NEEDS

Psychological

achievement
challenge
friendship
independence
learning
love
recognition
recreation
respect
security
self-expression
fulfilment
self-respect
sense of meaning

Physical

clothing
health
shelter
water
food

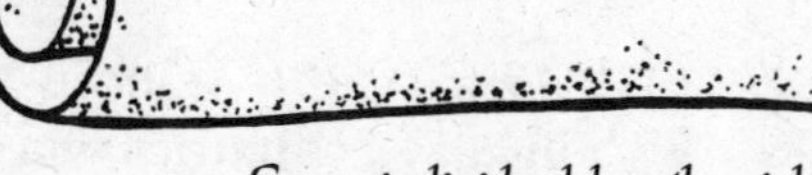

THE UNITED NATIONS DECLARATION OF HUMAN RIGHTS (1948)

Every individual has the right to:

Life
Liberty and security of person
Not be a slave
Not be tortured
Protection of the law
A fair and public hearing in the courts
Be presumed innocent until proved guilty
Freedom of movement and residence
Marry and found a family
Own property
Freedom of thought, conscience, religion
Freedom of opinion and expression
Freedom of peaceful assembly and of association
Seek and receive information and ideas
Take part in politics
Work
Fair wages and equal pay for equal work
Social security
A decent standard of living
Join a trade union
Rest and leisure
Education

All these rights are irrespective of any differences of race, colour, sex, language, religion, political opinion, social origin, property, birth.

❶ RIGHTS IN THE NEWS

(20 minutes)

Hand out a selection of newspapers to each of the original groups of 3 or 4; ask them to find as many stories as they can about the 11 situations they have just ranked. Ask the small groups to tell everyone else about these.

Alternatively, ask the groups to look out for stories of human rights abuses in the next week's news and to report back when they next meet.

❷ 'SAME RIGHTS FOR SEVERINA'

Arrange a showing of this 30-minute video from Christian Aid (see Resources Section), which explores human rights in Brazil. It powerfully demonstrates how democracy does not necessarily guarantee such rights and investigates the role of Christians in situations of oppression. Use the discussion material which comes with the video.

❸ JOIN AMNESTY INTERNATIONAL

The group will then be kept up to date about human rights abuses all over the world. It will also be given lots of action ideas – things members can do to really make a difference. (See Address Section at the back.)

And finally . . .

In its 1992 report, Amnesty International identifies 142 countries where abuses of human rights occur. Which country is the report describing here?

"About 90 Arab nationals were detained pending deportation on national security grounds, many of whom were prisoners of conscience. One prisoner of conscience . . . was imprisoned for 14 months." "Several people were killed in suspicious circumstances by the security forces . . . Detainees were reportedly ill-treated in police custody."

(Answer: The UK. The last two sentences refer to Northern Ireland.)

All human beings are born free and equal in dignity.

Article 1, UN Universal Declaration of Human Rights

Read Matthew 12:1-6

■ **What does this passage say about human rights?**

Leader:	Who will set us free? Who else can set us free?
ALL: (REFRAIN)	*JESUS, JESUS, WE'RE WAITING, WE'RE WAITING FOR YOU. YOU SAID YOU'D BE COMING, YOU SAID YOU'D BE COMING. DON'T LET US HOPE FOR NOTHING, DON'T LET US HOPE FOR NOTHING.*
Leader:	Who will open our eyes? Who else can open our eyes?
ALL:	REFRAIN
Leader:	Who will give us life? Who else can give us life?
ALL:	REFRAIN

O God of all youth, we pray to you:
We are young people, and we want to celebrate life!
We cry out against all that kills life:
hunger, poverty, unemployment, sickness, repression, individualism, injustice.
We want to announce fullness of life:
work, education, health, housing, bread for all.
We want communion, a world renewed.
We hope against hope.
With the Lord of history we want to make all things new.

Prayer written by a group of Brazilian young people

I have come so that they may have life and have it to the full.

John 14:14

10 To your good *health!*

Starter exercise:

WHAT IS HEALTH?

TIME

(15-20 minutes)

INSTRUCTIONS

— In groups of 3 or 4, ask people to make a list of their answers to the following questions. (Allow 7-10 minutes):

- **What makes you feel healthy?**
- **What makes you feel less healthy?**

— Ask people to share their answers with the whole group; write up the main points on the large sheet of paper in 2 columns: 'HEALTHY' and 'UNHEALTHY'.

— To what extent are the answers related to our western lifestyle? Do you think people from the Third World would give different answers?

YOU WILL NEED

large sheet of paper
marker pen

Main exercise:

A DECENT HEALTH SERVICE?

TIME

(30-35 minutes)

YOU WILL NEED

'List of Options', 1 photocopy between 2
large sheet of paper prominently displayed
marker pens and paper for everybody

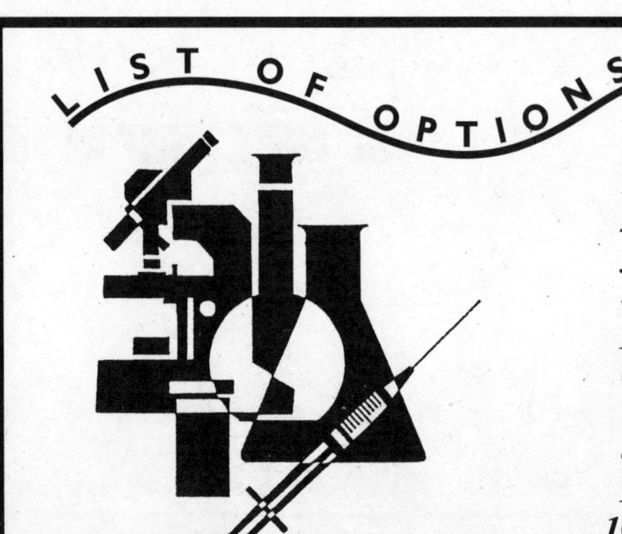

1. **Plentiful drugs**
2. **A large well-equipped hospital**
3. **Nutrition classes for mothers**
4. **A clean water supply for all**
5. **X-ray and scanning equipment**
6. **A good surgeon**
7. **Mobile health workers**
8. **Wholesome diet**
9. **Powdered baby milk for all new mothers**
10. **A psychiatrist**

INSTRUCTIONS

— Set the scene:

"You are health consultants and have been called in to advise a poor community in rural south India. The village is over 100 miles from the nearest town and the roads are terrible - dusty in the dry season; mud during the rains. Because the rains are unreliable growing rice can be difficult. The only source of water is the village well; even this sometimes dries up. Diseases caused by under-nutrition are common. Diarrhoea is a killer.

How could the health of this community be improved?"

HEALTH HEALTH HEALTH HEAL

— Split the group into pairs and give them each a 'List of Options'. Ask the pairs to decide how they would advise the community. Which are the 3 best and the 3 worst options? (Allow 10-15 minutes.)

— Meet back as a big group and hear the results of each pair's deliberations. On the large sheet of paper record people's choices: a tick for the best, a cross for the worst. Do this without comment.

CHRISTIAN AID/C. STEELE PERKINS

■ A paramedic pays a home visit, Bangladesh

NOTES FOR LEADER

CAFOD, Christian Aid and SCIAF would all stress the following:

OPTION

4 **A clean water supply for all.**	Most diseases in the Third World are easily preventable. Polluted water causes 80 per cent of the world's diseases, so clean water is therefore a priority.

CHRISTIAN AID/M. MURRAY

■ People take advantage of the new village pump, India

3 and 9

Nutrition classes for mothers

Another priority is basic health education, especially for mothers who are nearly always responsible for the family's nutrition. There is nothing better for babies than their mother's milk.

Powdered baby milk...

Powdered milk, while often aggressively advertised in the Third World by western companies, can in fact be dangerous. Many mothers cannot afford to make up the powdered formula to the correct strength – if they can read the instructions. And, if made up with unsafe water or unsterilised bottles, it can cause disease.

SOPHIE BAKER

■ **Pumping water for irrigation, India**

1 and 7

Drugs...

Health workers

Most fatal diseases in the Third World can easily be cured. Dehydration caused by diarrhoea is the biggest killer of under-5s, yet can be treated by a simple mixture of sugar, salt and clean water. This and other simple treatments can be administered by trained local health workers who visit the villages. Such workers can deal with over 90 per cent of Third World illnesses – without needing costly drugs to do so.

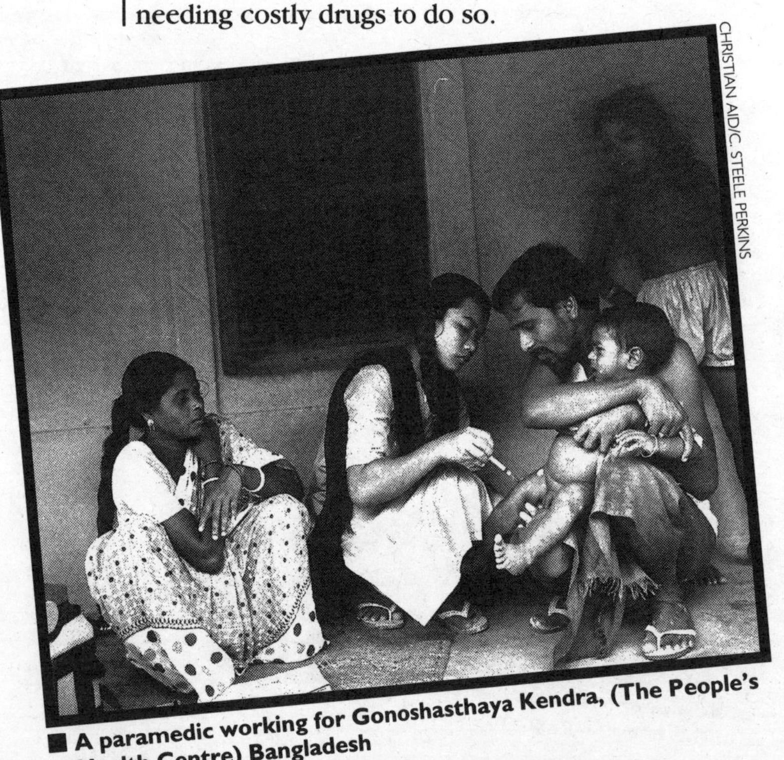

CHRISTIAN AID/C. STEELE PERKINS

■ **A paramedic working for Gonoshasthaya Kendra, (The People's Health Centre) Bangladesh**

2, 5 and 6

Hospitals, X-rays...

Big hospitals and highly sophisticated equipment are expensive to run and difficult to maintain in rural areas. They are also unnecessary for most diseases. Likewise, a good surgeon would be less beneficial than a local health worker.

8

Diet

Since the traditional diets of people in the Third World include less refined foods they are often very healthy. The important thing is to get enough to eat. Western diets are now believed to be linked to diseases like cancer and heart disease.

10

Psychiatrist

More necessary in western societies where stress and breakdown are often linked with life style and family patterns.

POINTS FOR DISCUSSION

— Having familiarised yourself with the 'Notes for leader', try to get the group to work out for themselves why small-scale community health care and prevention is so important. It is important not simply to say which answers are 'right' or 'wrong'. Therefore, only feed in the information from the notes gradually.

- **Why did people choose the options that they did? Get pairs who chose very differently to argue their respective cases.**
- **What illnesses did the pairs think were the biggest problems faced by their community?**
- **Are any options, however desirable, simply impractical?**
- **The kind of projects CAFOD, Christian Aid and SCIAF fund are based on options 3, 4 and 7. Why do you think this is? Are you surprised by any of these? Do you agree with them?**
- **CAFOD, Christian Aid and SCIAF would not be very likely to fund projects based on options 2,6 and especially 9. Why do you think this is? Are you surprised? Do you agree?**

A LOCAL HEALTH WORKER WRITES...

Jovinta Zuniga is a Mapuche Indian woman from rural southern Chile. She explains the difference her work has made to local communities:

"A few years ago, scabies and diarrhoea were very common in my area. At that time I was in a women's group. We knew something had to be done, but were not sure what. We heard that the local Methodist church was starting to train women in basic health care. To my surprise, the group asked me to go and do the training. It was hard work learning, but after a year I was commissioned and given my medicine box. Straight away I was able to make a difference. A simple preparation of sulphur and Vaseline is all it takes to get rid of scabies. The people in villages where scabies was rampant couldn't believe how easily it disappeared. An important part of my work is teaching people how they can avoid disease. To be honest, I still can't believe how much healthier and happier people have become — and it's me who has helped to change things!"

HEALTH FACTS

- Dehydration caused by diarrhoea kills over 8,000 children a day. A solution of salt and sugar in water can treat most cases and costs less than 5p to prepare.
- One death in 3 in the world is of a child under 5.
- 30,000 people die each day because of inadequate water supplies or poor sanitation.
- 1.5 million babies die each year because they are denied their mother's milk through the aggressive marketing of powdered milk in the Third World.
- Three quarters of all the diseases in the world could be prevented or quickly cured by the kind of primary health care described in Jovinta's story.

FOLLOW UP

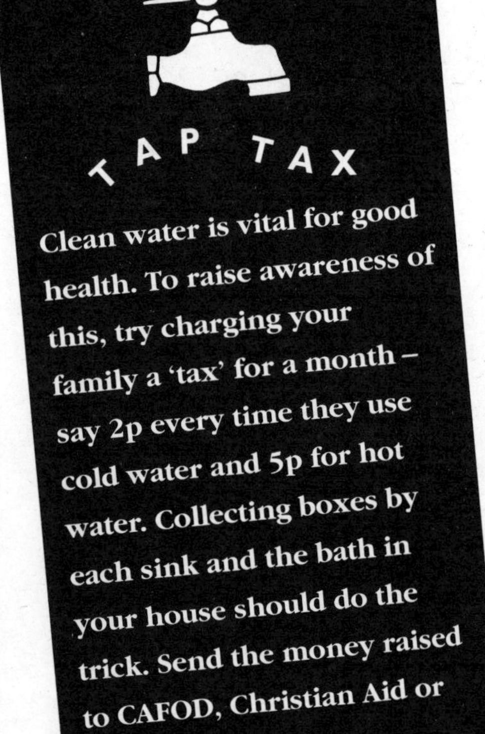

Baby Milk Action Coalition

In 1991, The General Synod of the Church of England backed the consumer boycott of a commercial product for the first time. The product was Nescafé, made by the world's biggest food company, Nestlé. The boycott was called because of Nestlé's promotion of dried milk as a substitute for breast feeding in the Third World. Nestlé was accused of supplying its product free to mothers until their own milk dried up and they were forced to start buying the Nestlé substitute or watch their babies starve.

If the group wants to learn more about the ways that western companies 'encourage' the sales of their powdered milk in the Third World, they should contact the Baby Milk Action Coalition which can provide lots of material on this subject (see Address Section at the back).

Find out about HIV/AIDS

HIV/AIDS is a worldwide phenomenon. In Africa its impact has been particularly catastrophic.

In 1992:

- **Of an estimated 10 million people with the HIV infection worldwide, around 6 million were in Africa.**
- **In central and eastern Africa, about 1 in 40 adults is HIV positive. In Uganda, the figure is more than 1 in 4 of the entire population.**
- **In Malawi, 23 per cent of pregnant women are infected with HIV. There is a possibility that their children will be born with the virus.**

— But HIV/AIDS is not just an African problem – it is estimated that 1 person is infected every 15 to 20 seconds somewhere in the world. The implications for development are disastrous. If your group wants to find out more about HIV/AIDS in the Third World, send off for further information on AIDS from CAFOD or Christian Aid (see Resources Section).

— Read out the following:

A traditional method of Christian prayer is to imagine yourself in a gospel story, meeting Jesus and seeing him in action. The key to this is:

Let your imagination run free – don't be held back by what you feel you 'ought' to think.

— Read Mark 10:46-52. Then read the following meditation slowly, leaving silences where the dots are. Gentle music in the background may help.

You are now going to imagine you are the blind beggar, Bartimaeus, whom Jesus healed outside Jericho. In order to do this, you must first take some time to get relaxed, so get into a comfortable position, close your eyes and very deliberately relax your muscles . . . If you find anywhere tense, relax it . . . Listen for a while to the sound of your own breathing . . . Don't change it, just concentrate on it . . . Can you hear or feel slight differences between each breath . . . ?

Now take time to imagine that you are Bartimaeus. . . a blind beggar, waiting by the side of the road . . . How does it feel sitting there . . . ? Is it comfortable or not . . . ? Now you hear the crowd getting nearer . . .

They reached Jericho; and as he left Jericho with his disciples and a large crowd, Bartimaeus (son of Timaeus), a blind beggar, was sitting at the side of the road. When he heard that it was Jesus of Nazareth, he began to shout and to say: "Son of David, have pity on me."

. . . Why are you shouting like this . . . ? What do you know about Jesus . . . ? How do you feel as you shout . . . ? Nervous? Scared? Excited? What . . . ?

And many of them scolded him and told him to keep quiet but he only shouted the louder: "Son of David, have pity on me." *How does it feel when people are scolding you . . . ? Why are they so cross . . . ? Why do you keep on shouting . . . ?*

Jesus stopped and said: "Call him here." *This is the first time you have heard Jesus' voice . . . What is his tone . . . ? How do you feel when you hear him taking your side . . . ?*

So they called the blind man. "Courage," they said, "get up; he is calling you." So, throwing off his cloak, he jumped up and went to Jesus . . . *What are your feelings inside as you go up to Jesus . . . ? What has happened to the crowd now . . . ? Have they gone quiet . . . ? What is the atmosphere like now . . . ?*

Then Jesus spoke, "What do you want me to do for you?" . . . "Master," the blind man said to him, "let me see again." *How do you feel as you ask Jesus for your sight . . . ?*

Jesus said to him: "Go; your faith has saved you." And immediately his sight returned and he followed him along the road. *When your sight returns what can you see . . . ? What does it feel like . . . ? What do you do? Jump around . . . ? Go quiet . . . ? Hug Jesus . . . ? What . . . ? What are your feelings about Jesus as you follow him along the road . . . ?*

Now slowly and in your own time, return to this room . . . don't rush, and when you're back don't move, just open your eyes . . . I'll let you know when everyone's back . . .

DEBRIEFING

When everyone's back, ask them what they felt. Did they find the exercise easy or difficult? Go through the meditation, asking them how they answered the various questions asked in the course of it. Encourage them to talk as Bartimaeus. What is the relationship between Jesus' kind of healing by faith and the medical skills of today?

Finally, point out that cataracts, one of the commonest causes of blindness, can be cured by a simple 20-minute operation costing only £8. Between 17-20 million people in the Third World suffer from cataract blindness. More information about this can be obtained from the organisation Sight Savers (see Address Section at back).

If the group found the exercise helpful, try doing the same thing another time with another gospel healing story - for example, the cure of the paralytic (Mark 2:1-12) or the woman with the haemorrhage (Mark 5:25-34).

Every man, woman and child should be in a position to choose a healthy way of life. To do this, they must be adequately informed on matters that have an influence on health: the environment, water, food, good habits and bad ones.

Dr Hiroshi Nakajima,
Director-General,
World Health Organisation, 1989

We want to create hope for the person with AIDS and acceptance in the hearts of the people. We must give hope, always hope, and remove the bitterness that harms them when they are avoided by everyone.

Mother Teresa of Calcutta

Lord, comfort the sick, the hungry, the lonely and those who are hurt and shut in on themselves, by your presence in their hearts; use us to help them in a practical way . . . Make us open to them and give us courage to suffer with them, and that in doing so we share with you the suffering of the world, for we are your body on earth and you work through us.

Michael Hollings and Etta Gullick from *The One who Listens*, McCrimmon

11 A matter of life and debt

AIM

The exercises in this chapter explore the causes and consequences of Third World debt

Starter exercise:

flip-chart
marker pen

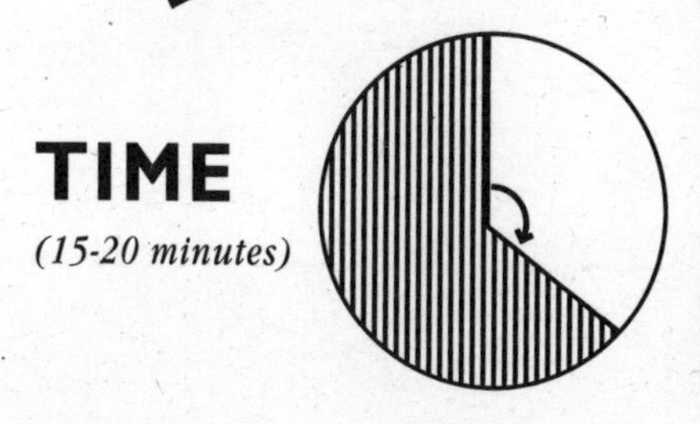

TIME

(15-20 minutes)

— Ask everyone in the group to stand up. Then read out the following list. If any statement applies to the family of any group member, s/he must sit down when it is read out.

1. **They have a mortgage.**
2. **They own anything bought on hire purchase.**
3. **They have used credit cards.**
4. **They do not have coin meters to pay for gas or electricity.**
5. **They have a telephone.**

— Announce that anybody still standing up is from a family with no debts. (If everybody is sitting down, feel free to feign surprise as theatrically as you like.)

BRIEF DISCUSSION

- What would happen if your family didn't pay its various debts?
- How would you feel when these things happened?
- Why might people be unable to pay their debts? List as many reasons as you can on the flip-chart.
- Which of these do you think are the debtors' fault?

Main exercise:

'A Matter of Interest' video (see Resources Section), TV and video player

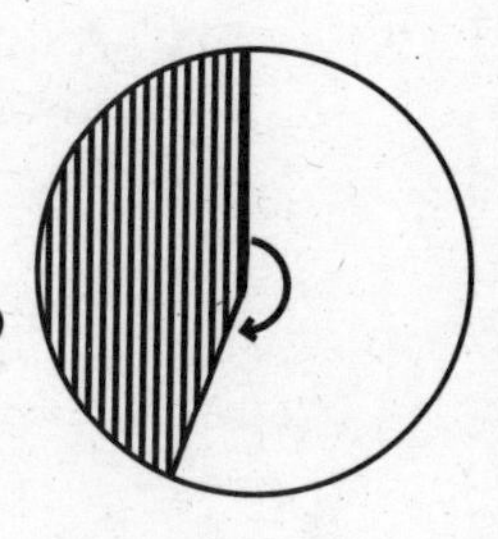

TIME

(30-35 minutes)

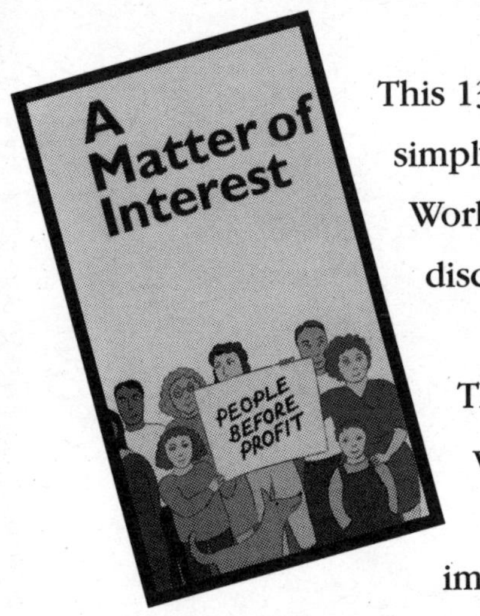

This 13-minute cartoon video explains very simply the origins and effects of the Third World debt crisis. It comes with its own discussion material.

The only tricky economic point in the video is the statement that devaluation of the currency causes the price of imports to rise. Ask the group to work out why this is, either before or just after watching the video.

AFTER THE VIDEO

— Ask people for their reactions:

■ **Which bits of it made them most angry? How much of it did they know about before? What were they most surprised by?**

— Do the following quiz. Feed in the multiple-choice options only if people are stuck. (Answers top of page 69)

WERE YOU PAYING ATTENTION?

Where did western banks suddenly get the extra money which they lent to Third World countries in the 1970s?

a) A pools win.
b) From the oil-producing countries following big oil price rises.
c) From the money invested following the privatisation of state-owned industries in Europe.

What is capital flight?

a) A particularly good air journey.
b) A down payment on a large loan.
c) Money taken out of a country and invested abroad with the aim of making a bigger profit.

What do the initials IMF stand for?

a) Institute of Mercenary Financiers.
b) International Monopoly Fanclub.
c) International Monetary Fund.

An interest rate is:

a) The number of times people change channels per hour of TV viewing.
b) the level of extra money people pay for the privilege of borrowing.
c) the speed with which a debtor repays a loan.

Who suffers most under IMF conditions?

a) The poor.
b) IMF officials.
c) People called Trevor.

What is the link between international debt and rainforest destruction?

a) Trees must be cut down to provide the paper needed for all the international reports on the situation.
b) Some banks accept repayment in the form of timber.
c) Third World countries earn money to pay off their debts by exporting timber and beef from once-forested areas.

QUIZ ANSWERS
1b; 2c; 3c; 4b; 5a; 6c

Follow up exercise:

THE BURDEN OF DEBT

TIME
(20-25 minutes)

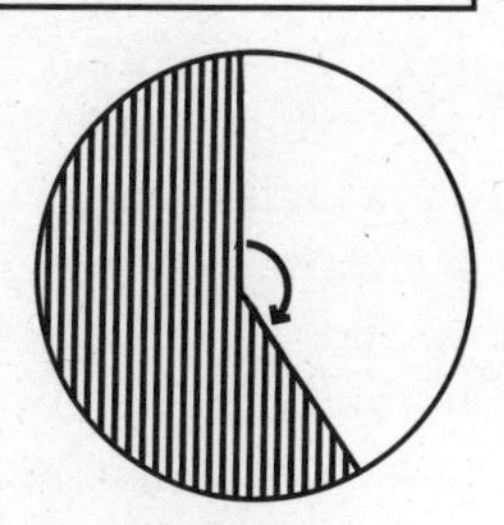

photocopies of Mercedes' story
two lists of options (see below)
flip-chart and marker pen

INSTRUCTIONS

— Read through Mercedes' story with the group.

THE STORY OF MERCEDES

Butuan is one of the main towns in the southern Philippines. It used to be prosperous, thriving on the timber felled in the surrounding forest for export. But the loggers were greedy and bulldozed everything in their path. The forest has now almost gone and many timber yards have closed. People fled into Butuan looking for work and many shantytowns have sprung up.

Mercedes, married with 5 children, lives in a rented hut. Her husband, a timber worker, is now unemployed and there is no social security so Mercedes has to provide for the family. She is a street-trader, selling home-made rice-cakes at the bus station. She finds it difficult to find the money to buy ingredients and fuel.

To help pay its debt, the Philippines government has had stringent policies imposed on it by foreign creditor governments, the IMF and the World Bank. In seeking to spend less and earn more, it has increased the price of basic foods and put new taxes on the kerosene needed to cook rice-cakes.

So, Mercedes and her street-trader friends were forced to borrow money or go bust. The banks were not willing to lend, so they went to a moneylender. For every 4 pesos she borrowed, she had to pay back 5 the next day. If she couldn't, she had to borrow more to make the repayments. The tiny profit on each day's work was swallowed up in repayments. And a bad day's trading could lead to a spiral of debt. What could she do?

CHRISTIAN AID/D. KNIGHT

■ **Two shantytown women taking part in loan scheme for street traders, Philippines**

— Split into 4s or 5s and ask each group to rank (best at top) the possible responses given to the following two questions:

1 WHY DID MERCEDES GET INTO DEBT?

a) She was stupid to get involved with a moneylender in the first place.

b) Men such as her husband just won't take responsibility for their families.

c) The Philippines government has messed up the economy – hence the high food prices and harsh new taxes.

d) The banks lent too much money irresponsibly to the former President of the Philippines, Ferdinand Marcos.

e) The IMF is cruel in insisting that the Philippines government increases taxes and food prices.

f) Europe's greed for tropical hardwood has led to the destruction of the forests around Butuan.

2 WHAT SHOULD CAFOD, CHRISTIAN AID AND SCIAF DO?

All 3 organisations exist to strengthen the poor. Which of the following options should they concentrate on? What might Mercedes ask them to do?

a) Send money for soup kitchens in the shantytowns so that people get one decent meal every day.

b) Help the community to set up a fund so that the women can borrow at rates they can afford.

c) Help those who are developing programmes to grow food on the severely eroded land that was formerly tropical rainforest.

d) Support groups in the Philippines seeking to prove that the debt is the responsibility of the ex-dictator Marcos – so the present government should not have to pay.

e) Press banks in the UK to stop demanding full repayment of the Philippines debt which is owed to them.

f) Lobby the UK government to ensure that policies agreed between the IMF and the Philippines government do not harm the poorest people.

— Meet back and hear what the groups thought. Mark their answers on the flip-chart and discuss the findings.

CAFOD, Christian Aid and SCIAF are involved in b) to f). Option a), which is only a short-term alleviation and not a solution, would not be done alone – as the debt crisis should be attacked from all sides.

GORDON STOWELL

If your group wants to find out more about debt and its consequences, why not:

Show either:

the 20-minute video 'Jamaica: No Problem', which shows the effect of the country's massive debt on Jamaican life. (See Resources Section)

or:

the 15-minute video extract 'Hell to Pay' from 'Land, Hope . . . and Glory?', in which Bolivian women talk very movingly about the effects of debt on their lives. (See Resources Section)

FOR STUDENTS

1. For more information on Third World debt contact Third World First (see Useful Addresses).

2. Find out more about the student boycott of Lloyds and Midland Banks because of Third World debt. Write to:

Lloyds and Midland Boycott
Manchester University Students' Union
Oxford Road,
MANCHESTER.
Tel: 061-275 2930

DEBT FACTS

- **In sub-Saharan Africa, one fifth of government spending goes in debt repayments. This is more than is spent on health and education combined.**
- **Nearly 1,400 children die EVERY DAY as a direct result of the debt crisis.**
- **Every year the Third World pays the West around £12 billion more than it receives in aid.**

(From *The State of the World's Children*, United Nations Children's Fund (UNICEF), 1992)

- **In Jamaica, the national debt is the equivalent of every man, women and child owing £1,000 to lending institutions in the West. The average wage in Jamaica is £300 a year.**

REFLECTIONS

Few scourges in human history can claim so many victims as today's debt crisis.

President Robert Mugabe of Zimbabwe, 1990

There is not enough soap in the world to make me clean again after what I have done to the poor on behalf of the rich.

Davison Budhoo,
former IMF employee

I have no hesitation in admitting that the banks do bear some responsibility for the debt crisis, simply through having lent too much.

Sir Kit McMahon,
ex-chairman of the Midland Bank

I don't like western solutions to the debt crisis – they kill too many people.

Javier Iguinez,
Peruvian economist

A QUICK DEBT BIBLE STUDY

Read Nehemiah 5:1-13

- **What are the main complaints of the people?**
- **Can you think of any modern parallels with their situation? (Clue! Compare v5 with the situation in the Philippines, where many people have to work abroad and where many women and young girls are forced into prostitution.)**
- **What is Nehemiah's reaction to what he hears? (vv 6-9)**
- **What is his solution? (vv 10-13)**
- **Is this solution possible in our own debt crisis?**

If you lend money to any of my people . . . you must not demand interest.

Exodus 22:25

12 There's only one Planet Earth

Warm-up exercise:

(20 minutes)

— On everybody's back stick a piece of paper with a different environmental issue written on it: loss of the ozone layer; pollution of rivers; acid rain; rainforest destruction etc.

— Tell everyone that they now have 15 minutes to find out what issue they are by going around the room asking other people questions about what is on their back. They must ask only questions which can be answered 'Yes' or 'No' and can ask each person just one question before moving on.

— When the time is up, go around the group and see how many people have guessed what they are.

— Explain that of these issues, the group is now going to concentrate on rainforest destruction by playing . . .

Preparing the game:

('Timber!' needs more preparation than many of the exercises in this book, but it is well worth it.)

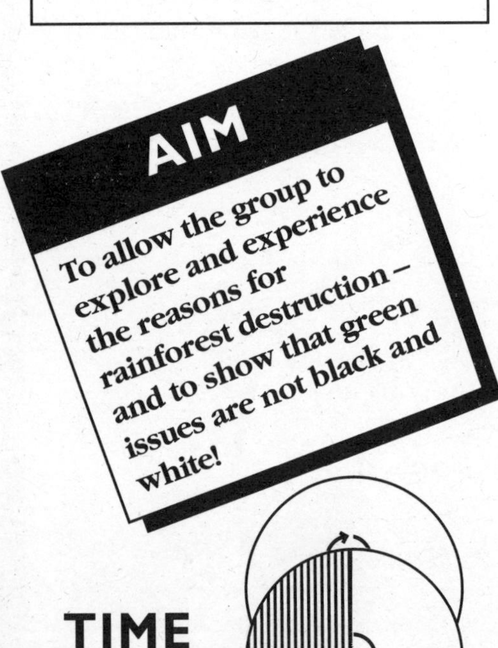

YOU WILL NEED

8 circles of the required number of chairs around the outside of the room
1 table in the middle of the room with 75 upturned paper cups representing the forest
whistle, pen and paper for leader
1 envelope per group containing:
- **1 background card per member (page 75-76)**
- **1 blank name badge per member**
- **pens**
- **('Background Information' for Forestwatch only) (page 77)**

Ideally 'Timber!' should be played with between 25 and 30 people – though it can be adapted. For 30 participants the suggested division is:

Group	Number
Burgerbeef Inc.	**4**
Forestwatch	**4**
Government resettlement team	**4**
Kopano tribe	**4**
Medico Ltd.	**4**
National Timber Company	**4**
Resettled people	**3**
River Basin Regional Council	**3**

NOTES FOR THE LEADER

(read these before starting the game)

1 Reforestation is carried out simply by replacing cups up to the maximum number stated. You should keep an eye on this process. Reforested cups should be marked with an 'R' to indicate that they are newly planted.

2 Don't be afraid of the strong feelings this game can unleash. Intervene only if necessary for reasons not linked to the game. Otherwise just observe.

3 It's a good idea to note down any particularly striking things you see or overhear. Mention these in the course of the debriefing. You may even want to draft in another observer as you will find a lot goes on during the game. Introduce them to the group at the beginning and explain that they will not interfere or help participants in any way. Ask these observers for their comments in the debriefing too.

RAIN FOREST RAIN FOREST RAIN FOREST

INSTRUCTIONS

◆ Divide participants into 8 groups, direct them to the circles of chairs. Introduce each of the groups.

◆ Read out the 'Background Information' (page 77) then give it to the Forestwatch group.

◆ Announce the following:

"The forest used to be considerably larger than it is now; all that remains of it is represented by these paper cups. An international conference to decide what should be done about the destruction of the forest will take place sometime in the future. Nobody knows exactly when, but all groups are advised to prepare their case to put to the conference.

You now have 10 minutes in your groups to read through and discuss the background cards in the envelope in front of you. Also in the envelope are name badges for everybody. Please fill in your name and group and put the badge on while you are discussing. Go!"

◆ During the 10 minutes, go round and check that the groups understand their role.

— Announce:

"The 5-minute intervals will be indicated by a whistle. On hearing the signal those groups with a timber requirement should remove the appropriate number of 'trees' (ie cups) from the forest. Certain groups might also want to find out more about each other's plans, and negotiate or form alliances. This first blow of the whistle indicates the beginning of a 15-minute period to do all of this. Don't take any trees on this first blast."

CHRISTIAN AID/SALOMON CYTRYNOWICZ

■ **The logging industry threatens large areas of rainforest around the world**

◆ Blow the whistle and spend the 15 minutes observing, overhearing, BUT NEVER INTERFERING WITH, what is going on. (Once the game is under way you should ignore all enquiries and complaints.) Don't forget to blow the whistle every 5 minutes.

◆ At the end of this period, announce a 5-10 minute 'taking stock' period. No tree felling is allowed and people must stay in their groups discussing what they have learnt and what they plan to do next.

◆ At the end of this, announce that the international conference will take place in 10-20 minutes. All groups are asked to have a 2-minute statement ready. A whistle blow now indicates the resumption of tree felling and negotiations between groups.

◆ The exact timing of the conference is up to you and should depend on how the game's going and how much of the forest remains; if possible, it should take place just as the last trees are removed. In the meantime, observe as before, blowing the whistle every 5 minutes. If the forest disappears call the conference immediately.

◆ Blow the whistle and announce that the conference is about to begin. Say that you (the leader) are now a United Nations adviser sent to hear all the arguments. Allow the groups a couple of minutes to collect their thoughts then call them together facing you and chair the meeting. Ask each group in turn to put its case, asking for clarification if necessary. After hearing all the statements, make a fake exit, promising to send your report 'in due course'.

The game is now finished.

CHRISTIAN AID/SALOMON CYTRYNOWICZ

■ **Cutting down hardwood trees, Brazil**

CHRISTIAN AID/SALOMON CYTRYNOWICZ

■ **Logging is big business in Brazil**

BACKGROUND CARDS

BURGERBEEF INC

You are a branch of a large transnational corporation which operates in over 30 countries. Your parent company is based in Dallas, Texas. Because of the increased demand for beef products in western fastfood markets, you have had to search for new ranchland outside the USA. This has brought you into the forest where you have now been ranching for 6 years. It is an expensive operation, burning down trees and converting the land into pasture - especially as the soil is exhausted after 2-3 years and new land has to be found. However, because the land is cheap and the beef can be sold expensively, profits are high. The operation also provides employment for local people in an area with an expanding population.

Your employees in the forest have had occasional skirmishes with the Kopano tribe and rifles are now supplied as standard equipment. There is also increasing competition for the forest's land and resources. You are therefore developing an aggressive purchasing policy, with attractive incentives for the national government in return for unrestricted access to the forest.

TIMBER REQUIREMENTS

For your forest clearing operation you need to cut down 3 trees every 5 minutes of the game.

If you wish to speed up your operation, this requirement can be increased with the agreement of at least 1 other group in the forest. You can voluntarily reduce your requirement at any time.

FORESTWATCH

You are a representative of an international pressure group which is concerned about the worldwide destruction and exploitation of the tropical rainforest. Your unit must try to persuade the various groups in the forest to reduce their timber requirements and promote a reforestation programme.

Your campaigning is non-violent but you persistently lobby; providing public information and education for people living in the forest. You also want to convince the commercial exploiters of the long-term effects of what they are doing. Use the information sheet you have been given to try and do this.

If you are successful in establishing a reforestation programme, which must be carried out by 1 or more of the groups that is cutting down trees, you can replant up to 2 trees every 10 minutes of the game. (The National Timber Company already has a reforestation programme which should replace 1 tree every 10 minutes.)

GOVERNMENT RESETTLEMENT TEAM

You are responsible for carrying out the resettlement programme in the forest. This was one of the main policies for which your government was elected and has been running for 6 years. It started because the cities had become grossly overcrowded as the rural poor flocked in searching for work. Work was hard to find, and the shantytowns became a national and international disgrace, rife with disease and poverty.

The resettlement programme is, you believe, humane and generous. It provides purpose-built accommodation for poor families with electricity, drainage and running water, and also gives them a small plot of land on which to grow crops. The men can find employment logging or ranching, and roads have been built to connect the communities to nearby cities. The programme is expensive, with only a little money coming back in the form of rent, but it is felt to be the only solution to the problem of the cities, so will be expanded. The government wants to remain on good terms with Burgerbeef Inc, but doesn't want to get a bad reputation abroad as a destroyer of the forest.

TIMBER REQUIREMENTS

For the resettlement programme to continue, you need to cut down 2 trees every 5 minutes of the game.

If you wish to speed up the programme, this requirement can be increased with the agreement of at least 1 other group in the forest. You can voluntarily reduce your requirement at any time.

KOPANO TRIBE ('THE FOREST PEOPLE')

Your tribe has been living in the forest 'since people began', according to the stories handed down through the generations. The tribe's survival is due to the skill of its people in using the forest's vast resources for food, shelter and medicine. You practise a shifting agriculture - using a patch of land for a few years before moving on to another, thereby allowing the original land to recover and trees and plants to grow again. The tribe also needs firewood.

In recent years your tribe's peaceful co-existence with nature has been disturbed by the appearance of foreigners who have done a lot of thoughtless damage - either by chopping down the sturdiest trees, or by setting fire to large areas of the forest. Moreover, diseases unknown to you before have killed many of your people. So have the weapons of the foreigners. The tribe's leaders would like to retaliate but there is disagreement between those who advocate peaceful protest, in keeping with tribal philosophy, and those who want to use violent means.

TIMBER REQUIREMENTS

For your firewood, you need 1 tree every 5 minutes of the game. This requirement can be increased with the agreement of at least 1 other group in the forest. You can voluntarily reduce your requirement at any time.

MEDICO LTD.

You are a branch of a transnational corporation, based in London and operating in over 20 countries. Your company specialises in drugs for use in surgery, many of which are made from substances found only in forest plants. Many of these are already in use, but you are also undertaking an extensive research programme to explore the healing potential of thousands of other plants about which little is currently known. Many medical experts believe that cures for many of the West's most common ailments, including heart disease and cancer, may be found among such plants. There would be an incalculable contribution to medical knowledge if these cures were discovered - and also to your company's profits.

Hence, you have become very concerned about the increasing destruction of the forest which is eliminating valuable plant species, both known and unknown. Your parent company has given you the financial backing to begin campaigning among the other users of the forest in order to slow down the rate of destruction.

NATIONAL TIMBER COMPANY

You are a thriving state-owned company, employing 1,500 people, supplying the ever-increasing demand for hardwood from western Europe and especially Japan. You have a 'selective logging' policy in the forest, cutting down only those trees which are of the right quality to satisfy market demands. However, these trees are often closely surrounded by other, unwanted, trees which have to be removed to get the logging equipment to the good trees. Recently, you have had to take on less experienced loggers from among the resettled people, who are not so careful about the job. They are needed, though, as the orders are still rolling in.

Thinking about the future, you have begun a reforestation policy of planting some commercially viable and fast-growing species of trees in cleared areas. It is in these areas that your foresters need to be particularly vigilant as there have been instances of 'tree poaching' by members of the Kopano tribe and others.

TIMBER REQUIREMENTS

For your logging operation you need to cut down 2 trees every 5 minutes of the game. If you wish to expand your operation, this requirement can be increased with the agreement of at least 1 other group in the forest. You can voluntarily reduce your requirement at any time.

Under the reforestation programme, you can replant 1 tree for every 10 minutes of the game.

RESETTLED PEOPLE

You are one of 1,500 people who moved 5 years ago from a poverty-stricken slum area of the capital city to a newly cleared area of the forest. You moved voluntarily, because life in the city was so hard and the government promised your a new life - lovely new houses, clean air, clean running water, land to grow crops - and a job with the National Timber Company.

All of these promises were initially fulfilled. However, as more people arrived, jobs were not so easy to get. Also the yield of crops has dropped recently as the soil in the cleared areas has become exhausted. Your family is therefore once more entering the cycle of poverty you thought you'd escaped forever. As a result, you have become bitter, feeling you have been dropped in a remote area by a government desperate to solve the problems of the overcrowded cities. At least there, there was a lively community. Here, you feel isolated in a barren wilderness.

Some of the resettled people are also angry at the exploitation of the forest by various outside interests; others among you are arguing that you too should be clearing areas of the forest to provide fertile land for crops. You will need the agreement of at least 1 other group to do this.

RIVER BASIN REGIONAL COUNCIL

You represent the 500,000 people who live in the River Basin region, some 300 miles downstream from the forest. Until 1978, your people had led comfortable lives, growing rice as a cash crop. Since then, flooding, once very rare, has become an increasingly common problem. Five times in the last 10 years the river has burst its banks after heavy rain and whole villages have been destroyed - with many deaths. Farming is now very difficult because the unpredictability of stream flows has resulted in the rice having either too much or too little water. Poverty has increased alarmingly among your people, and many have been forced to look for work in the already overcrowded cities.

It has long been rumoured that the clearing of large areas of the forest has caused the flooding. Rainfall, for example, has not increased significantly in the last 15 years and the silting up of the river, which leads to bank-bursting, is thought to be caused by the soil washed into the water after trees are cut down. You have therefore been asked by your community to find out more about the 'strange goings-on' in the forest and to see if you can solve the problems of the River Basin area. At present, though, exactly what you should do is not clear and with more and more trees being cut down, time is running out . . .

BACKGROUND INFORMATION

1 A few thousand years ago a rainforest belt covered 14 per cent of the earth's land surface. Humankind has already destroyed half of that, most of the damage being done in the last 200 years - especially since 1945.

Latin America has 57 per cent of the remaining rainforest (Brazil alone has one third). SE Asia and the Pacific islands have 25 per cent; Africa has 18 per cent.

2 Tropical rainforests are being destroyed faster than any other part of the natural world. According to a US National Academy of Sciences survey, over 50 million acres (the area of England, Scotland and Wales combined) is destroyed or seriously degraded every year. At the current rate, almost one fifth of the remaining tropical rainforest will have been destroyed or severely degraded by the year 2000.

3 The major causes of rainforest destruction are:

■ slash-and-burn clearance for shifting agriculture; the cleared area is then used to grow crops for 2-3 seasons before it is abandoned.

■ steady clearance for fuelwood (ie firewood and charcoal); one third of the world's population relies on fuelwood for heating and cooking.

■ organised national/international logging operations for economically useful timber.

■ organised extensive clearing for cattle grazing. The land is cheap (particularly in Latin America) and a high price is paid for lean meat by US hamburger manufacturers.

■ government resettlement policies, aimed at reducing the pressures of overcrowding on the cities and at making 'economic' use of the land.

4 Between 40-50 per cent of all types of living things - 5 million species of plants, animals, insects - live in tropical rainforests, though they cover less than 2 per cent of the globe.

This includes people: anthropologists estimate that in 1500 the Amazon basin had a population of 6-9 million. In Brazil today there are less than 200,000 Indians; about half the 230 tribes who lived in Brazil at the turn of the century are now extinct.

AFTER THE GAME

The debriefing is very important. You should try and allow the participants to express their feelings as freely as possible while still keeping order. Use the following questions to help participants reflect on their experiences during the game:

■ **How did you feel about the role you were asked to play?**

■ **How did the 'local people' (Kopano tribe, resettled people, River Basin Regional Council) feel about the 'outsiders' in the forest?**

■ **What did those working in the forest think about the people who lived there?**

■ **What was your group's attitude towards conservation of the forest?**

■ **Did any group increase its timber requirements during the game? Were any groups persuaded to reduce theirs?**

■ **Do transnational corporations have a right to cut down large areas of forest? Whose interests are they serving?**

● Report back what you saw and heard as you watched the game.

● Questions for participants to discuss as themselves (not in the role they played):

■ **What can be done to prevent the destruction of the forests?**

■ **What have you learnt from playing this game?**

TIMBER! (this is a slightly shortened version) was devised by Graham Pike, International Institute for Global Education, University of Toronto.

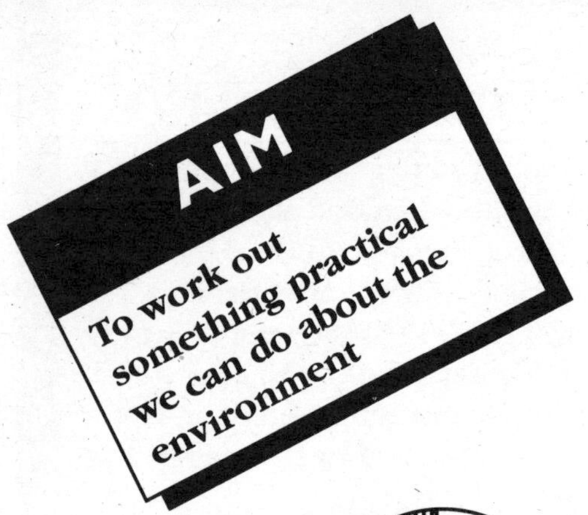

Follow up exercise:

pen and large piece of paper for each pair

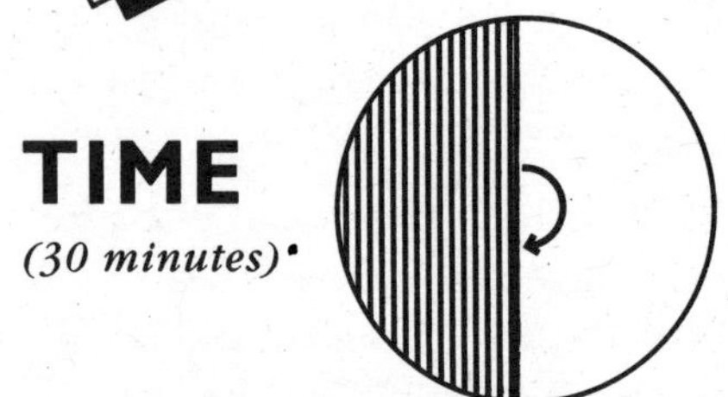

INSTRUCTIONS

— Split the group into pairs.

— Ask each pair to:

Choose one environmental problem (eg rainforest destruction). Write it in the middle of the piece of paper and draw a circle round it.

■ **In a circle around the problem, write down all the causes of it that you can think of (eg land cleared for hamburger companies). Put all the causes in their own circles and join these to the central problem with lines.**

■ **Now, and this is where it gets a bit tricky, around each cause write down all the causes of that cause (eg the western love of fast food) put them in circles and join them to the primary causes.**

■ **Think of one of the causes of the causes and then make a list of all the things that can be done to alleviate this problem. Tick those things on the list that you can do to help.**

— Back in the big group, hear what people have decided they can do as a group, and as individuals, resolve to do at least one of them.

REFLECTIONS

FURTHER SUGGESTIONS

For more ideas of environmental activities with young people, see the Resources Section at the end of this book.

JOEL KAUFFMANN

Where do we humans fit into the scheme?

There is a lot of debate about what should be the relationship of human beings to the rest of creation - the environment.

Genesis 1:26 has been used to suggest that we have the right to do whatever we like with creation. It is this attitude which has allowed us to be so destructive of nature. But the Bible has more angles on the matter than this.

Read these passages:

(which also says that human beings are made in the image of the Creator.)

(who is superior in creation?)

(with whom does God make a special relationship?)

(what sort of place does humanity seem to have here?)

Matthew 6:26-30

— For each of these passages, how would you describe the relationship of human beings to the rest of creation? Is it one of domination, sharing, superiority, interdependence, care, equality, or what?

— Discuss your own understanding of this, and how the present day threats to creation are forcing us to rethink our views.

How might people in the Third World see things?

For Third World people, whose cultures are often more in tune with nature than our own, poverty often forces them to destroy the environment in order to survive.

"We in the Third World are destroying our environment. We cut down the wood to make fuel to cook. We cut the wood to sell to the cities to make our living. In 15 years there will be no trees left in Ghana . . .

"I tell you: there is only one way to solve the threat to the environment. Poverty must be eliminated. How? You must have less. We must have more. You must sacrifice to give. You must give out of love."

Bernard Guri,
Ghanaian agriculturalist

Enjoy the earth gently
Enjoy the earth gently
For if the earth is spoiled
It cannot be repaired
Enjoy the earth gently

Yoruba poem, West Africa

13 Political *Persuasions*

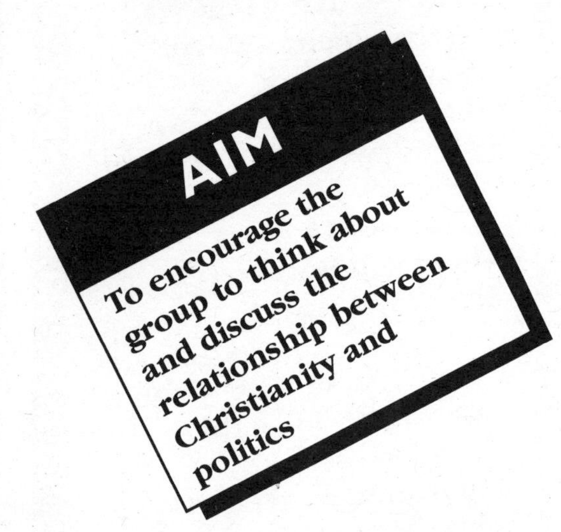

Main exercise:

NOW WHAT DO I SAY?

YOU WILL NEED photocopies of the dialogues below

INSTRUCTIONS

- **Split into pairs and give each pair a copy of one of the dialogues to act out and conclude as they choose.**
- **Allow 10-15 minutes for the pairs to discuss and rehearse their dialogues.**
- **Meet back in the big group. Ask a pair of volunteers for each of the dialogues to act it out together with what they decided to say next.**
- **After each one, discuss who the group thought was right and why.**
- **Finish by discussing how the group expects change to come about in the world.**

TIME

(30-90 minutes, depending on how many of the dialogues below you choose to do)

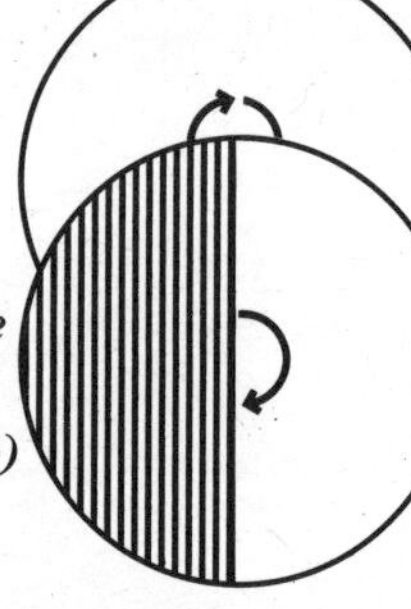

DIALOGUES

1 THE IMPOTENCE OF BEING EARNEST?

Situation: Paul, 17, and his father have just been watching a TV report on famine in Africa:

PAUL: I can't believe it. The 1990s and there's still people starving in the world. There must be something we can do.

DAD: Not really, son. I've been watching programmes just like that for 30 years now. I mean I'll gladly bung them a fiver, but I don't expect it'll change much.

PAUL: But, Dad. We must do more than that. The whole world needs to be changed. People in the West must learn to share what they have with the poor.

DAD: Oh, here we go. Well, I've worked for what I've got. It just wouldn't be fair to take my money away from me. Anyway, I don't notice you complaining when I slip you cash from time to time, or give you good presents at Christmas. I can't see you living in a shack, I must say.

PAUL: Well, Dad, I promise you now that, when I'm older, I'm never going to be rich while there's poverty in the world. It's against scripture and it's immoral.

DAD: Yes, I used to think like that when I was young. You'll grow out of it.

PAUL: No Dad . . .

2 NOTHING TO DO WITH CHRISTIANITY?

Situation: Judy has just given a talk to a parish group about the Christian development agency she works for. The agency helps poor people in the Third World who are organising into groups to demand their rights and to struggle for a fair deal. It also tries to change attitudes in this country. Mrs Crowther, the chairperson of the parish council, approaches Judy over the coffee afterwards:

MRS CROWTHER: Sweet talk, Judy, but I must say I couldn't really agree with some of what you were saying.

JUDY: Oh! Which bits?

MRS CROWTHER: Well, most of it really. I mean the agency's meant to be Christian isn't it?

JUDY: Yes.

MRS CROWTHER: Yet a lot of what you do seems to have nothing to do with Christianity. I agree that we should be helping unfortunate people, of course, but all that stuff about demanding their rights, changing attitudes here and trying to get our government to change its policies towards the Third World. To me, I'm afraid, that rather smacks of politics – and we all know that one shouldn't bring politics into religion.

JUDY: But Mrs Crowther . . .

3 TELLING IT LIKE IT IS?

Situation: David, a priest and university chaplain, is visiting Mike, a fellow-priest and old college friend, in his new parish. The two are having a pub lunch following Mike's Sunday morning service.

MIKE: Cheers, David. It's good to see you again, I must say.

DAVID: You too, Mike. Though I must say, I was quite shocked by your sermon this morning.

MIKE: What do you mean?

DAVID: Well, you were such a radical at college, and this morning's Gospel seemed to present a golden opportunity to preach some hard-hitting things about rich Christians who never challenge the status quo because it suits them so well. You know, all the things we used to talk about back then.

MIKE: It's all right for you, David, in that university chaplaincy, surrounded by idealistic young people. The people in this parish are all doing very nicely, thank you. If I preached the full Gospel about lifestyle and wealth, they'd all just go somewhere else. The church would be empty in a month.

DAVID: But, Mike that's not the point, surely . . .

4 THE MARX OF THE TRUE CHRISTIAN

Situation: Sally, a Christian, and her non-Christian friend, Simon, are discussing religion:

SIMON: Sally, you're a Christian right?

SALLY: Uh-huh.

SIMON: And I've heard you say before that Christians must be concerned with social justice, with seeing that the world's goods get shared out fairly. True?

SALLY: True.

SIMON: But isn't that what Communism tried to do – and look what happened to that. You may not like the fact, but it does seem that people like to get rich, they don't want to share. Human nature being what it is, your 'political Christianity' is just too naive ever to work.

SALLY: But, Simon. I believe . . .

I HAVE A DREAM-- WHERE CREATURES ARE NO LONGER DIVIDED JUST BY THE COLOR OF THEIR SKIN, BUT BY CLASS AND IDEOLOGY. WHERE THE RICH THIRD OF THE WORLD...

1 SO WHERE DO YOU STAND?

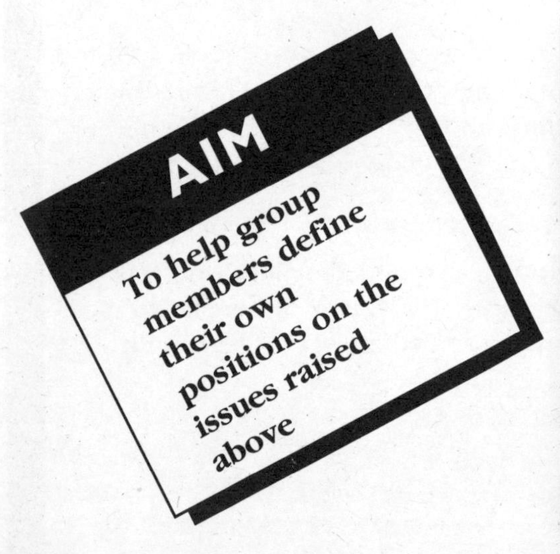

CHRISTIAN AID/S. FRANKLIN

■ Christians in the Philippines protesting against the government, 1987

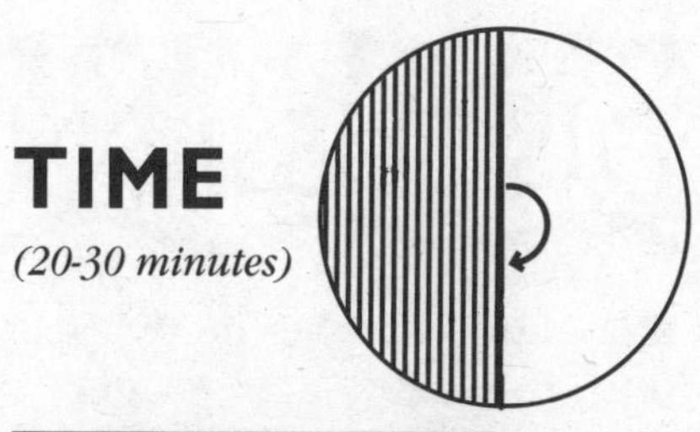

TIME

(20-30 minutes)

INSTRUCTIONS

— Ask the same pairs to discuss the following statements, decide which of the following reactions they have to each one, and why:

STRONGLY AGREE — AGREE — NOT SURE — DISAGREE — STRONGLY DISAGREE

— Meet back in the big group and discuss what the pairs decided.

— Ask the pairs to guess which statement is a direct quotation from the Bible: it's number 1 (Romans 13:1). Are they surprised by this? Does it make any difference to their reaction to it?

YOU WILL NEED

1 photocopy of the statements and a pen per pair

STATEMENTS

1. **Christians must obey the government.**
2. **The only way to change society is to change individuals.**
3. **No Christian should ever vote Conservative.**
4. **The primary task of the Christian is to evangelise.**
5. **Politics always involves compromising your beliefs to get things done. That is why Christians, who can never compromise the Gospel message, must not get involved.**
6. **The Church in this country doesn't speak out loudly enough on social issues.**
7. **If Jesus came back today, he would antagonise the rich and powerful just as much as he did the first time around.**
8. **Christians in this country should form their own political party.**

CHRISTIAN AID/S. FRANKLIN

■ **A mass protest after the killing of five farmers, Manila, the Philippines.**

2 THINKING ABOUT CHARITY

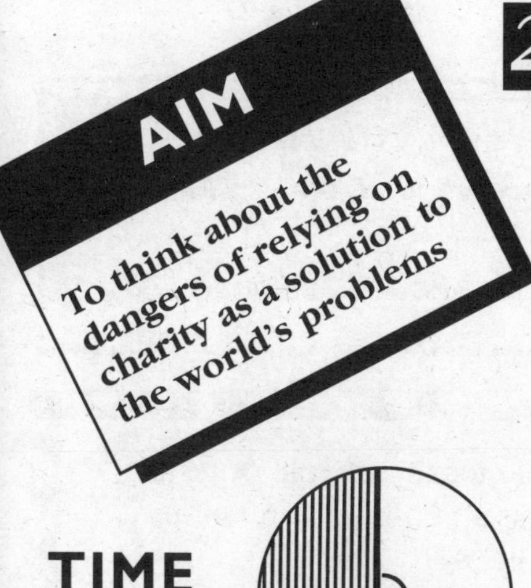

TIME

(20 minutes)

A PARABLE – by Brian Wren

There was once a factory which employed thousands of people. Its production line was a miracle of modern engineering, turning out thousands of machines a day. But the factory had a high accident rate. Day after day, men and women came out of work with squashed fingers, cuts, bruises. Occasionally someone was electrocuted or crushed to death.

Enlightened people began to see that something needed to be done. First on the scene were the churches. An enterprising minister organised a small first-aid tent outside the factory gate. Soon, with the backing of local parishes, it grew into a properly built clinic, able to treat quite serious cases. The local Rotary Club and Chamber of

Commerce then became interested and the clinic grew into a small hospital, with modern equipment, an operating theatre and a full-time staff of doctors and nurses. Several lives were saved. Finally, the factory management, seeing the good that was being done, and wishing to prove itself enlightened, gave the hospital its official backing and a small annual grant. It also donated an ambulance to speed serious cases from workshop to hospital ward.

But, year by year, as production increased, the accident rate continued to rise. More and more men and women were hurt or maimed despite everything the hospital could do.

Only then did some people begin to ask if it was enough to treat people's injuries, while leaving untouched the machinery that caused them.

POINTS FOR DISCUSSION

- **Did the churches do the right thing in the first place? Later on?**
- **What would you advise the churches to do now? The factory management? The factory workers?**
- **What does this parable say about the churches and politics? About charity? What parallels can you draw with other situations you know about?**
- **Do you agree with the points the parable is making?**

3 ARRANGE A VIEWING OF 'YONDER PEASANT'

A 22- minute cartoon videostrip which explores the Christian response to world poverty, through a fantasy parable based on the story of Good King Wenceslas. The video comes with its own discussion material (see Resources Section).

When I give food to the hungry, they call me a saint. When I ask why the poor have no food, they call me a communist.

Dom Helder Camara, Brazilian bishop

I am puzzled about which Bible people are reading when they suggest religion and politics don't mix.

Archbishop Desmond Tutu, South Africa

It would have been impossible for the people of Jesus' time to have thought of him as an eminently religious man who steered clear of politics.

From *Jesus before Christianity* by Albert Nolan (Darton, Longman and Todd)

An African development worker has said:

"Imagine that you are by the bank of a river, when you notice a child in the water. You jump in and rescue him, but as you are getting your breath back, you notice another child in the river. You rescue her, and then see another one. Eventually, you look around and see a man on a hill. He is throwing children into the river. That is what my work is like."

Oscar Wilde (1854-1900) on charity:

Why should the poor be grateful for the crumbs that fall from the rich man's table? They should be seated at the meal and are beginning to realise it.

(From *The Soul of Man under Socialism*)

CONSERVATIVE

"It is my contention that Conservative policies derive from a view of how God's world works, which is nearest to what I discern the Gospels to proclaim."

John Selwyn Gummer, Conservative MP

Labour

"Christian principles are also the basic perspectives of British socialism and therefore Labour Party members, whether religious or not, can accept Christ's teachings as basically their own. In working for a Labour government with socialist objectives they also are accepting the Christian idea of creating God's Kingdom."

Eric Heffer, Labour MP

Liberal Democrats

"The application of Christian principles has led me to choose liberalism."

Alan Beith, Liberal Democrat MP

14 But what can WE do?

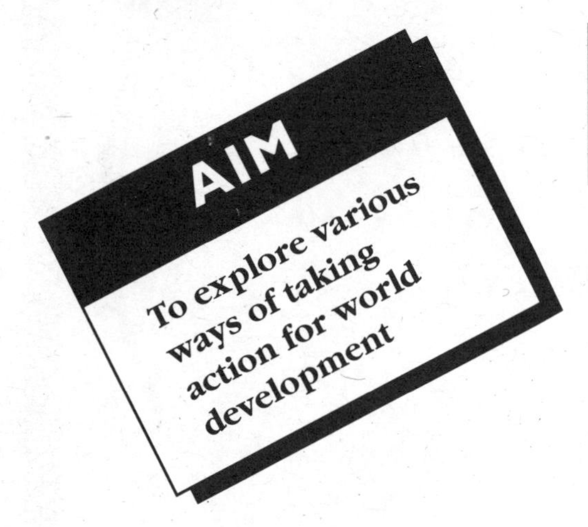

large chart to write up answers
pens
photocopies of the options opposite
marker pen

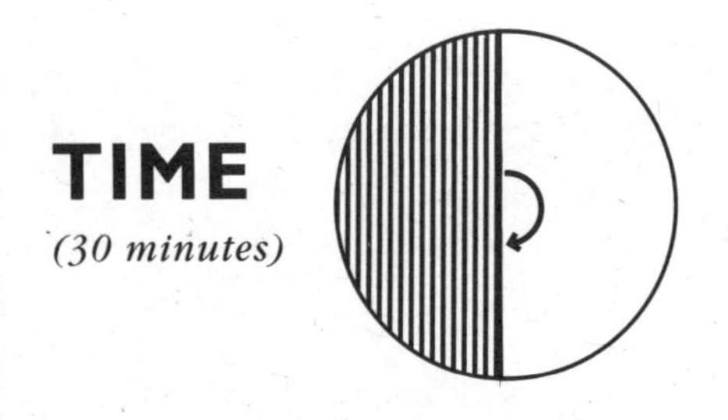

TIME
(30 minutes)

INSTRUCTIONS

— Split the group into 3s or 4s.

— Read out the following:

> **"Often we know what is wrong with the world. We hear of poverty, injustice and war. We want to do something, however small, to make the world fairer. But what?**
>
> **"Your job in this exercise is to answer that question. Here are 10 possible answers to the question: 'But what can we do?' In your group decide which are the 3 best and 3 worst answers. Each group will then report back with their decisions and the reasons for them. You can, of course, also come up with 'good' answers of your own."**

— Allow 15-20 minutes for the groups to decide and then meet back for the discussion (see 'Notes for leaders' opposite).

■ Hear from each small group what they decided and why. On the chart mark the options with a tick for 'best' and a cross for 'worst'. Do all this without comment.

■ Note the winners and losers. Point out anything of interest like options with both ticks and crosses, or where all but one group were in agreement. In such cases ask the disagreeing group(s) to defend their choice(s).

■ Point out the things in the 'Notes for leaders' opposite. Are the groups surprised by any of them? Try to make these points as gently as possible and as a matter of interest, not as 'the right answers' now that the groups have had their go.

1 Everybody here to sponsor a child in the Third World.

2 Everybody here to find out which western companies are responsible for gross injustice in the Third World, to publicise this and boycott their products.

3 The group to support projects overseas which strengthen the poor in their struggle for a full life.

4 Everybody here to find ways of living as simply as possible (perhaps not buying records, computer games or many clothes – even getting your parents to cut your hair) and giving the money saved to the poor.

5 People here to persuade their local church to find a suitable project to which to send a van, and to send it with 'gift from the people of (name of church)' on the side.

6 Sadly, there's nothing we can do. Human nature cannot be changed.

7 Campaign for income tax to be increased in all tax brackets by 0.5 per cent, with all the extra money to go straight to overseas aid.

8 Make a concern for the poor central to the Sunday services at church.

9 Everybody here to dedicate themselves to finding out the causes of poverty in the Third World, and to tell others what they find out.

10 The only way of bringing about real change in the world is to convert everybody in it to Christianity.

NOTES FOR LEADERS

This is an exercise primarily designed to encourage discussion. There are not necessarily any right or wrong answers. However, CAFOD, Christian Aid and SCIAF do have jointly held perspectives on the options given. Here are some of them - partly for information and partly as material for further discussion.

OPTIONS

1 CAFOD, Christian Aid and SCIAF do not run child sponsorship schemes. (Nor does Oxfam.) We could all increase our incomes if we did, but we believe such sponsorship is not the best way forward for the Third World. It singles out individuals for help, it can encourage patronising feelings of 'looking after' poor people and it is very costly to administer.

3 This sums up the aims of CAFOD, Christian Aid and SCIAF.

4 This may well be the most scriptural answer of the 10. Did it win? Or was it dismissed as unrealistic? Does its scriptural status make any difference to the group?

6 This probably stood out as the obviously 'wrong' answer in a publication from 3 aid agencies. But perhaps we all believe it more than we like to admit. It is always interesting to look for traces of this attitude in what is said about the other answers.

9 Not to be underestimated. People in the Third World often stress how much they'd like people in the West to understand the reasons for global poverty.

10 It is a sad but undeniable historical fact that Christian countries and societies have never been fairer or gentler than non-Christian ones. Why is this?

FOLLOW UP

At the risk of sounding brutal, it is best if the follow-up to this exercise takes the form of calling the group's bluff – suggesting they do whatever it was that they decided they should! See Chapter Eighteen for practical tips on some of the options. Group members could even make written pledges, and perhaps make these the basis of 'The Service of Dedication' in Chapter Nineteen.

Is not this the sort of fast that pleases me – it is the Lord who speaks – to break unjust fetters and undo the thongs of the yoke, to let the oppressed go free, and break every yoke, to share your bread with the hungry, and shelter the homeless poor, to clothe the people you see to be naked and not turn away from your brothers and sisters? Then will your light shine like the dawn and your wound be quickly healed over.

Isaiah 58:6-7

Take the case of people who have never done a single good act but claim that they have faith. Will that faith save them? If one of the brothers or one of the sisters is in need of clothes and has not enough food to live on, and one of you says to them, "I wish you well; keep yourself warm and eat plenty," without giving them the bare necessities of life, then what good is that? Faith is like that: if good works do not go with it, it is quite dead.

James 2:14-16

15 *EATING* and *THINKING*

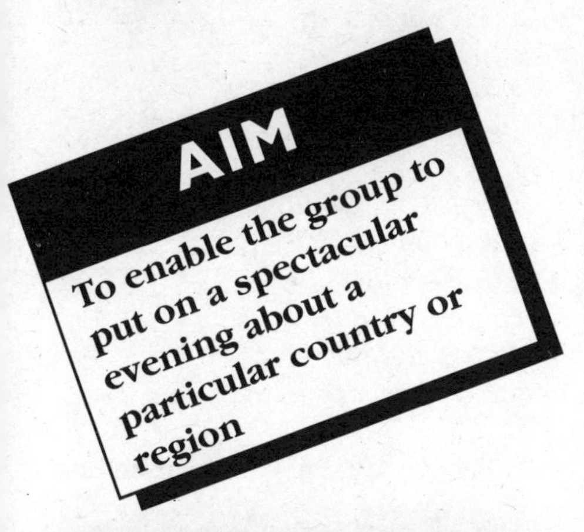

Putting on an evening focusing on one country is a highly effective way of getting the group's message across to the rest of the church or to another local youth group. Three frameworks for such evenings are given in this chapter. These are only suggestions for you to develop as creatively as you wish. Certainly, if you know of good speakers on countries or if your church has members with links with other countries, then do use them instead.

SOME TIPS

■ A good structure for this sort of evening is to serve some food from the place concerned, then to have a relevant speaker or video which leads on to a time for questions and/or discussion, and finish with a time of prayer.

■ Try and find some music from the region and play it as people arrive and depart. Ambitious groups could even build in a time for dancing.

■ Decorate the room with posters and objects from your focus country.

■ Ask speakers to bring along any clothes and objects that they have - and be willing to teach people some local games or dances.

■ Try and involve anybody from the focus country who lives nearby. Even if they don't want to be speakers, they might have music, decoration, fashion, games and dance ideas. Don't forget overseas students in the area - many will welcome a chance to chat about their country, and to hear about yours.

■ Many of the exercises from other parts of this book could be used instead of a speaker or video.

■ Whatever you decide to do, your local CAFOD regional organiser, Christian Aid area co-ordinator or the SCIAF development education organiser (numbers in the phone book) will be happy to help.

■ Recipes from various countries, including several in this chapter, can be found in *The Food Book* (New Internationalist, by Troth Wells, Oxford) and *Recipes from around the World* (Oxfam). Both addresses are at the back of this book. Rice is the basis of many of the meals mentioned here - a small cup of dried rice is enough for one person.

■ Prayers from around the world can be found in *Bread of Tomorrow* (Christian Aid) and *Celebrating One World* (CAFOD).

■ Good publicity is crucial for the success of the event. Put up posters and make announcements in church well in advance. You might think too about selling tickets after Sunday services.

CHRISTIAN AID/D. K. CREVANCE

■ **Cooking the evening meal, Koolnaykampatti village, India**

WHAT YOU CAN DO:

1 To help your Indian evening go with a swing, why not try and find some local people who can

- do some Indian dancing
- demonstrate how to put on a sari
- show and explain some Indian art?

2 Show the video 'The Tiger and the Oxen', which provides a good introduction to some of the issues of rural development in India. It lasts 28 minutes and comes with its own discussion material (see Resources Section).

3 Play the 'Paper Bag Game', a simulation game for 10-35 people which gives participants a powerful sense of what it's like to be locked in the struggle for survival in Calcutta (see Resources Section).

BADAMI MURGHI (CHICKEN WITH ALMONDS)

Serves 4

4 chicken breasts, skinned and cut into small pieces
4 tbsp oil
3 garlic cloves, crushed
1 tsp ginger
4oz/120g almonds
2 tbsp lemon juice
4 tbsp orange juice
2 tbsp coriander leaves, chopped
1/2 tsp nutmeg
salt and pepper

1 Brown chicken on all sides in hot oil.
2 Add remaining ingredients, except lemon/orange juices and coriander leaves. Mix thoroughly so meat and almonds are well covered with spices. Cook uncovered over a fairly hot heat for about 10 minutes until chicken is cooked.
3 Just before serving, pour in lemon and orange juices. Stir well. Serve hot with rice and garnished with coriander leaves.

LENTIL (DHAL) CURRY

Serves 4

6oz/170g lentils	*5 bay leaves*
4 small onions	*1/2 tsp cummin*
2 cloves garlic	*2 tsp salt*
chilli powder	*2 tbsp oil*

1 Chop 2 onions and garlic

2 Add washed lentils, chopped onions and garlic to 1 pint lightly salted water. Bring to boil. Simmer for 30 minutes, until mushy. Add more water if necessary.

3 Chop remaining onions and fry in oil until soft. Add bay leaves, chilli powder (to taste) and cummin, and fry lightly. Remove bay leaves.

4 Add mashed lentils and mix thoroughly while reheating.

5 Serve with boiled rice and yoghurt.

For greater authenticity, the dishes should be eaten with your fingers. Poppadoms or curried chips (see opposite) can be used as 'dippers'!

CURRIED CHIPS

Serves 4

6 medium potatoes
2-3 cloves garlic, crushed
1 tsp tumeric
1 tbsp sesame seeds
oil
salt

1 Heat a heavy pan over a medium heat and toast sesame seeds without oil. As they cook, they will jump and turn golden. Shake the pan so that they don't stick or burn.
2 Cut potatoes into chips and soak in water for 30 minutes. Drain and leave to dry out.
3 Heat enough oil to shallow fry the potatoes. Add salt. Cook for 15 minutes, stirring frequently.
4 Add tumeric and mix well to spread colour evenly.
5 When chips are nearly done, add garlic and toasted sesame seeds. Mix well and serve.

CHRISTIAN AID/MAURICE RYDER

■ **Food being cooked and sold at a pavement stall, Calcutta**

COCONUT CANDY

Makes 15 pieces

3/4 cup/180ml evaporated milk
3 oz /100g desiccated coconut
3 oz/85g sugar

1 Pour evaporated milk into a pan and add sugar. Heat gently, stirring all the time. When boiling, turn down heat and simmer until milk has reduced by half.

2 Add coconut and continue stirring until mixture sticks together in a ball. Remove from pan and transfer to a greased shallow dish or toffee tray. Spread evenly, using the back of a spoon.

3 Leave mixture to cool and cut into pieces

PRAYERS AND REFLECTIONS FROM INDIA

O God our Father, you have taught us that to enter the kingdom is hard and the way narrow. You have taught that to be a member is like paying the price for a unique pearl for which we must sacrifice many other treasures. Lord, open our ears that we may hear your voice in the midst of the babble of many voices that deafen us. Loosen the bonds that tie us to lesser things and give us the liberty to grasp at the one thing that is of real worth.

By Canon Subir Biswas, from *Lord, Let me Share*

For 2 voices:

A: So often in a city when a crisis occurs, people pass by saying: "It's not my responsibility." When you go to government departments, so often you hear the same words: "This is not our responsibility."

B: But you, Lord, have made us responsible for each other: for the neighbour, the stranger. This is the glory of your kingdom, you have put us in relationship, you have made us responsible with you. Help us, Lord, never to disown that responsibility. Help us never to forget that you are in all things and all things are in you. This day, help us to see you in everyone – and to take responsibility.

By Canon Subir Biswas, from *Lord, Let me Share*

BRAZIL

WHAT YOU CAN DO:

1 Try and find someone locally who can teach you some Latin American dances – the rumba, the samba and (for brave groups!) the lambada. Failing this, just put the music on and go with the rhythm!

2 Show the video 'The Same Rights for Severina'. This 26-minute video explores the effects of poverty in Brazil, and what people there are doing to overcome them. It comes with its own discussion material (see Resources Section).

RECIPES

FEIJOADA SIMPLES (BLACK BEANS WITH MEAT)

Serves 4

3/4lb/340g black beans, soaked overnight
1lb/450g stewing beef
4 rashers bacon
4 highly seasoned pork sausages
2 tbsp oil
1 large tin tomatoes
3/4 pint stock
dried basil
seasoning
Worcester sauce
1 clove garlic

1 Dice meat and onion. Chop bacon and fry until brown. Transfer to casserole dish.
2 Crush garlic and fry with pork sausages. Add tomatoes, a pinch of basil, stock and a dash of Worcester sauce.
3 Strain the soaked beans and add to mixture. Mix all ingredients with meat and add seasoning.
4 Cook in a slow oven (Gas 3 or 325°F) for 2 hours.
5 Serve with rice.

JOFRE MASCENO

■ **Washing up, Goania, Brazil.**

CREME DE ABACATE (AVOCADO CREAM)

Serves 6

3 large ripe avocados
2-4 tbsp fresh lemon juice
1 tbsp sugar
6 lime or lemon slices for garnish

1 Cut avocados in half and remove stones. Carefully scoop out flesh and mash with a fork. Keep the skins.
2 Add some lemon juice and sugar and beat until smooth. Taste; add more juice or sugar if desired.
3 Pile avocado cream into each half skin, garnish with a slice of lime or lemon. Chill in fridge before serving as a dip with raw carrot, celery sticks or tortilla chips.

MOQUECA (FISH STEW)

Serves 4-6

2lb/900g white fish fillets
3 tomatoes, sliced
1 lemon
1 chilli, cut finely
2 tbsp oil, preferably coconut oil
2 medium onions, sliced
6oz/150g shelled shrimps or prawns
fresh parsley, chopped
salt and pepper

1 Cut lemon in half and rub fish with it.
2 Heat oil in a shallow pan and cook onions and chilli until soft. Add tomatoes, fish, shrimps or prawns, lemon juice and salt and pepper to taste. Cook over a high heat for 1 minute, then turn off heat, cover pan and leave to stand for 1 hour.
3 After 1 hour, warm pan again and allow contents to simmer for a few minutes until fish is soft. Garnish with parsley and serve with rice.

BRAZILIAN PRAYERS AND REFLECTIONS

Come Lord
do not smile and say you are already with us.
Millions do not know you and to us who do, what is the difference?
What is the point of your presence if our lives do not alter?
Change our lives, shatter our complacency.
Make your word our life's purpose.
Take away the quietness of a clear conscience.
Press us uncomfortably.
For only thus that other peace is made, your peace.

Dom Helder Camara from *The Desert is Fertile* (Sheed & Ward)

Leader: Alleluia
All: Alleluia
Leader: Jesus, Word of God,
brother who speaks
truth to his brothers
and sisters,
give us your new
freedom.
Free from profit and
from fear,
we will live in gospel;
we will shout in gospel:
Alleluia
All: Alleluia
Leader: No power will silence
us. Alleluia
All: Alleluia
Leader: Against the orders of
hate
you bring us the law of
love.
In the face of so many
lies
you are the truth out
loud.
Amid so much news of
death
you have the word of
life.
After so many false
promises, frustrated
hopes,
you have, Lord Jesus,
the last word,
and we have put all our
trust in you. Alleluia
All: Alleluia

From 'Misa dos Quilombos', by Pedro Casadáliga (tr. Tony Graham, Christian Aid)

Help us to see in the groaning of creation not death throes but birth pangs;
help us to see in suffering a promise for the future,
because it is a cry against the inhumanity of the present.
Help us to glimpse in protest the dawn of justice,
in the Cross the pathway to resurrection,
and in suffering the seeds of joy.

Ruben Alves, Brazil

WHAT YOU CAN DO:

1 African music is very easy to dance to. In fact, music from Zimbabwe and South Africa is very hard not to dance to! Why not get hold of some (available from most good record shops) and end the evening with a mini African disco.

2 Show the video 'Africa: Our own story'. This 20-minute video looks at Africa through African eyes and comes with its own discussion material (see Resources Section).

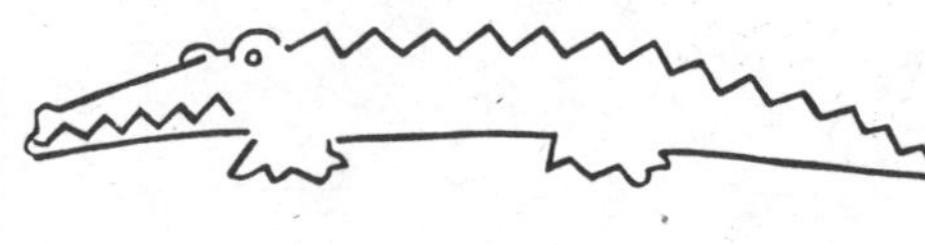

MENI-MENIYONG (SESAME SEED STICKS) (FROM MALI)

Serves 4

3oz/100g sesame seeds
1 cup honey or sugar
4 tbsp margarine

1 Toast sesame seeds in shallow pan without oil until they jump about and turn golden. Shake pan so they don't stick or burn. When ready, put to cool on one side.
2 Heat margarine in heavy pan. Add sugar or honey. Stir continuously until mixture caramelises.
3 Pour sesame seeds into warm mixture and stir in thoroughly.
4 Transfer mixture to a flat tin. Shape into sticks as it cools by cutting or rolling. Coat mixture with more sesame seeds.

CHRISTIAN AID/J HARTLEY

■ **Fatou Thiam sieves flour for cooking, Nganda, Senegal**

CHICKEN A LA MOAMBE (CHICKEN WITH PEANUT SAUCE) (FROM ZAIRE)

Serves 6

3lb/1.5 kilo chicken, skinned and cut into joints
4 tbsp oil
4 tbsp tomato paste
1 medium can tomatoes, chopped
1 tbsp lemon juice
1/2 cup/60ml water
2 tbsp peanut butter
salt and pepper

1 Brown chicken pieces on each side in hot oil, pour off excess oil and leave chicken in pan.
2 Mix tomato paste in a bowl with chopped tomatoes, lemon juice and water. Pour over chicken pieces. Stir gently and cover. Simmer for 30-40 minutes or until the chicken is cooked. Add more water if too dry.
3 Remove chicken pieces, place in a serving dish and put in oven to keep warm. Pour sauce into a bowl, add the peanut butter, salt and pepper to taste and mix well. Spoon this over chicken, stir gently so all pieces are coated and return dish to the oven for a further 10 minutes before serving with rice.

RED KIDNEY BEAN STEW (FROM KENYA)

Serves 2-4

8oz/225g tin of red kidney beans
1 onion, chopped
2-3 tbsp oil
3 large tomatoes, chopped
11/4 cups/300ml milk
a little stock or water
handful of fresh parsley, chopped
salt and pepper

1 Mash half beans in a bowl.

2 Heat oil in a heavy saucepan, add the onion and cook gently until transparent. Add tomatoes and cook for 2-3 minutes.

3 Mix onions and tomatoes with mashed beans. Gradually pour in enough milk to make a thick sauce and return to the saucepan. Add remaining unmashed beans. Increase heat and bring to the boil, stirring so that it does not stick.

4 Lower heat, cover and simmer gently for 10-15 minutes. Stir frequently. The sauce should be fairly thick, but more milk or water can be added according to taste.

5 Before serving, add salt and pepper to taste. Spoon stew over rice and garnish with parsley.

AFRICAN PRAYERS AND REFLECTIONS

From the cowardice that dares not face new truth
From the laziness that is contented with half-truth
From the arrogance that thinks it knows all truth,
Good Lord, deliver me.

Prayer from Kenya, ed John Carden in *Morning, Noon and Night* (Church Missionary Society)

O God:
enlarge my heart
that it may be big enough to receive the greatness of your love.
Stretch my heart
that it may take into it all those who with me around the world
believe in Jesus Christ.
Stretch it
that it may take into it all those who do not love him.
And stretch it
that it may take in all those who are not lovely in my eyes,
and whose hands I do not want to touch;
through Jesus Christ, my saviour, Amen.

Prayer of an African Christian from *With all God's People: The New Ecumenidcal Prayer Cycle* (World Council of Churches, Geneva 1989)

CHRISTIAN AID/MAGGIE MURRAY

■ **A Segon courtyard kitchen, Mali**

Open my eyes that they may see
the deepest needs of people;
move my hands that they may feed the hungry;
touch my heart that it may bring warmth to the despairing;
teach me generosity that welcomes strangers;
let me share my possessions to clothe the naked;
give me the care that strengthens the sick;
make me share in the quest to set the prisoner free.
In sharing our anxieties and our love,
our poverty and our prosperity,
we partake of your divine presence.

The Rev Canaan Banana the first President of Zimbabwe, from *The Gospel according to the Ghetto* (Mambo Press, 1981)

16 ACTION ROUNDUP

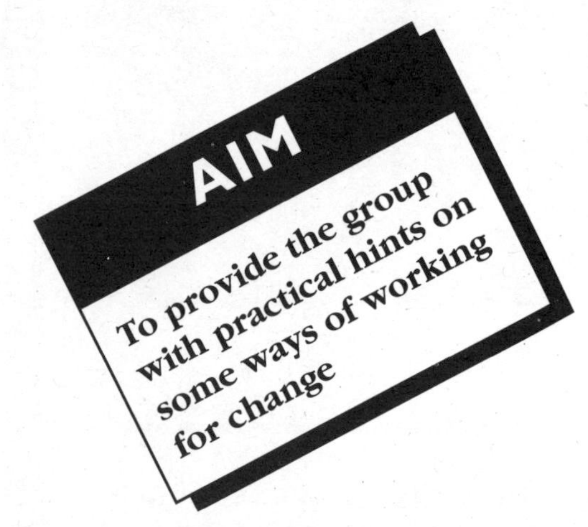

1 Continuing your own education

It's not necessary to be an expert on global history and economics to work for change. Being well informed, however, is a great help. Clearly people are more likely to listen to you if you know what you are talking about. This means reading the newspapers (the serious ones, that is!); watching the news and relevant documentaries on TV; and receiving regular information from organisations whose concerns you share.

As a starter, invite local representatives of the organisations you're interested in to speak to your group and bring along resources (see Addresses Section at the back of the book).

JOEL KAUFFMANN

2 Widening the circle

The more people there are who know about an issue, the more they bring pressure for change. Why not suggest that your group shows a video or runs a session with another youth group, or older people from your church. Alternatively, you could put on an event to which group members invite friends from school, college or work. (See Chapter Fifteen for more ideas for such events.)

CHRISTIAN AID/PETER DEVLIN

■ Collecting for Christian Aid Week

3 Going Public

Activities in the street with the general public can be very effective, but they do need careful planning. You might consider:

■ **Collecting money – contact the local representative of CAFOD, Christian Aid or SCIAF and get tins and stickers. Don't forget to get permission from the police and the shop you're standing in front of.**

■ **Increasing the educational impact of your collecting by giving out leaflets as you rattle the tins. You could write and design the leaflets.**

CHRISTIAN AID/E. CATLEY

■ A young sponsored swimmer notches up the lengths

■ **Busking with collecting tins and leaflets. Music will always draw a crowd. If anyone in the group has other skills, like juggling or magic tricks, use these too.**

■ **Performing simple street theatre. Design you own sketch based on one of the issues you have been exploring. You could attract a crowd by busking or juggling and then perform your sketch. Explain to the crowd what is going on and follow this up by handing round a petition for people to sign.**

TIPS ON STREET ACTIVITIES:

- **Make all movements and gestures exaggerated so that spectators and passers-by can't miss them. Wear bright colours or unusual clothes.**
- **Maximise the impact of any particularly spectacular events by informing the local media (see below) and handing out leaflets.**
- **Always inform the local police in advance about any event that is likely to draw a crowd and check on its legality.**

CHRISTIAN AID/ELAINE DUIGENAN

Racing for justice - lively and original events are more likely to catch the interest of the local press

4 Using the media

Make full use of local papers, radio and TV. Their reporters are always on the look out for unusual events, and media coverage will help your cause enormously. Let them know what you're doing by sending a press release.

Take photos of events and send them with a covering note to CAFOD, Christian Aid and SCIAF as well as church newspapers and magazines (see Addresses Section at the back). Such photos need to be of good quality. Check in advance whether the papers prefer colour or black and white photos; slides or prints.

HOW TO WRITE A PRESS RELEASE

- Write PRESS RELEASE at the top.
- Type on only one side of A4 paper in double spacing.
- Choose a simple, snappy heading which summarises your story.
- Explain who is doing WHAT, WHERE, WHEN, HOW and WHY.
- Keep paragraphs short – 3 sentences maximum.
- Include quotes; these give more weight to what you are saying.
- Don't forget to give the name of your group.
- Write ENDS at the end of the press release and put the date.
- Under ENDS give the name, address and telephone number of someone available to answer enquiries.
- Check for any mistakes and send it to 'The Editor'.

5 Money Raising

"Here's my contribution but . . . er . . . er . . . no information, thanks"

Raising money is a great way of getting the group to pull together and the money is always needed for work overseas. Do make sure that the group and donors know why they are raising money. In short, think educationally: give out leaflets, have thought-provoking posters around, set up a book-stall. Other points:

- **Feel free to think up new and imaginative money-making schemes but don't be afraid to settle for the old tried and trusted ones like sponsored walks, jumble sales and discos.**
- **Local shops are often very generous in donating prizes to raffles for a good cause.**
- **Always try to serve fairly traded tea and coffee at your events and provide leaflets explaining why. (See Chapter Six.)**
- **If you are raising money in a public place inform the local police in advance.**
- **Always tell the local media your plans.**

RICH/POOR MEAL

This is a particularly good way of raising both awareness and money. What you do is:

a) Sell tickets in advance for, say, £1. Each ticket entitles the bearer to either a rich or a poor person's meal. On arrival, guests take a slip from a hat which will indicate whether they are to get a slap-up, 4-course meal or a small bowl of rice. Two thirds of guests get the rice. The group, perhaps with family help, should do the catering, the waiting on the rich, the doling out of rice to the queuing poor.

b) Arrange the room so that the rich have plenty of space in the centre, with the poor crowded around the edges.

c) A chairperson or MC should explain what is going on and draw the parallels with our world where two thirds of people go hungry every day.

d) After the meal, or when the rich are on their dessert, introduce a speaker or video on world development.

e) End with a time of prayer.

f) Don't forget to have a stall with more information on the issues that the guests have experienced.

CAFOD, Christian Aid and SCIAF have free leaflets with lots of fund-raising hints and suggestions.

FUND RAISING FUND RAISIN

6 Put your whole 'art' into it

There are many creative and artistic things that can be done to spread the group's message. So, why not:

- Run a poster competition – involving local schools and art groups.
- Run a song competition – perhaps even get a DJ from local radio to help promote it.
- Ask a local theatrical group to prepare a drama on one particular issue and premiere their efforts at a charity evening.
- Make a huge collage about an issue that concerns the group and display it in your local library, a friendly shop window or the town hall. (Agree the display place before you begin work.)
- Make striking banners and hang them in your church.

CHRISTIAN AID/ELAINE DUGENAN

7 Action through your MP

MPs really do read and take notice of letters from their constituents - and they nearly always reply. Make your initial letter well informed and courteous, and if you feel that the reply is unsatisfactory follow up with further but still courteous points. If the correspondence continues for a while, why not invite your MP to talk (and listen) to the group about an issue you have been looking at? Alternatively, some of the group could go along to his/her surgery.

If you do not know your MP's name, ring 071-219 4272, say what your postcode is, and they will tell you. The address for all MPs is House of Commons, London, SW1A 0AA.

8 Other letter writing

Letter writing is not necessarily the most glamorous of activities, but it is very effective and the replies you get are always illuminating. People/organisations you might consider writing to include:

a) Companies or banks whose policies in the Third World you disagree with. In this case, it is vital that your group is very well informed as such organisations often reply with very plausible defences of their actions. Send letters to the managing director or chief executive, by name if possible.

b) Local papers. Address letters to the editor and keep them brief, clear and simply argued. Editors tend to be impressed by young people concerned about issues so put the ages of the writers at the end of the letter. If it's from the whole group, stress that it is a youth group.

If possible, send a simple leaflet to explain the issue in more detail in case the paper wants to follow it up.

c) Your MEP on issues where you think European Community policy is important. Check your local library for names.

d) Political prisoners. Do this through Amnesty International (see Addresses Section at back), which can supply names, stories and ideas about what to say.

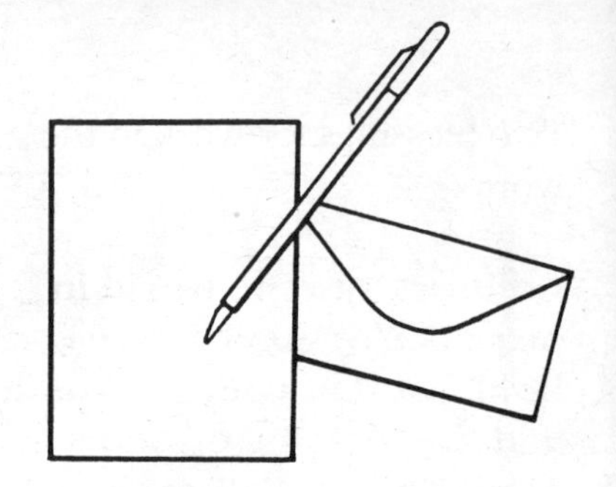

 Petitions

If you are collecting names for a petition, don't necessarily use a clip-board – everybody does that. Get something unusual for people to sign: a huge, well-designed poster, a cheque or, on trade, a colossal banana. The group also needs to be well informed as people who are asked for their signatures will want to know more and may argue a different point of view.

Make handing it in a real publicity stunt – eg take it direct to your MP (let the him/her know in advance), and inform the local media.

10 Celebrities

ASK THEM TO COME TO EVENTS OR TO DONATE PERSONAL MEMORABILIA AS PRIZES.

Involve people of influence in your campaigns – the mayor, local bishops and church leaders, local sports personalities, people who appear on local television and any national (or international) celebrities you may be lucky enough to live near. Ask them to come to events or to donate personal memorabilia as prizes.

Remember that having celebs on your side can be very helpful, even if they don't do very much. Quite famous people sympathetic to the cause are often happy to let you use their name as a patron if they know there will be little work involved for them. In these cases, tell the celeb concerned when you write initially that their name is all you need.

When your group is campaigning away very busily, don't forget to surround your actions with prayer.

Let every word be the fruit of action and reflection. Reflection alone without action or tending towards it is mere theory . . . Action alone without reflection is being busy pointlessly. Honour the Word eternal and speak to make a new world possible.

Dom Helder Camara (From *The Desert is Fertile*, Sheed & Ward)

Two blessings for work in the world:

Go forth into the world in peace; be of good courage; hold fast that which is good; and the blessing of God Almighty, the Father, Son and The Holy Spirit, be upon us and remain with us for ever.

Amen

An Act of Commissioning, from Bangalore, India. From *Morning, Noon and Night*, ed. John Carden, (Church Missionary Society)

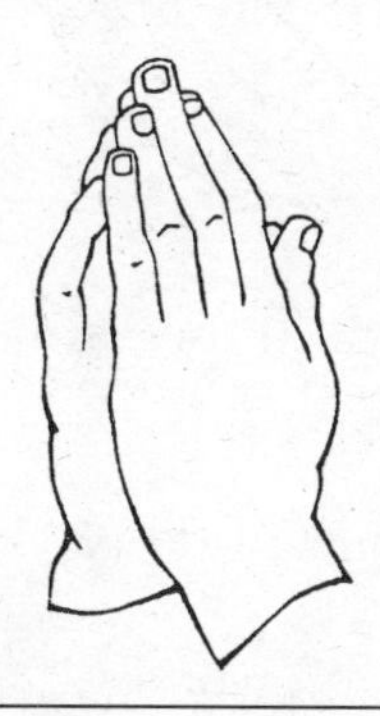

Leader: As we prepare to leave
and embrace the challenges
of our lives and our world,
let us ask for God's blessing.

May God bless us with strength
to seek justice.

ALL: AMEN

Leader: May God bless us with wisdom
to care for our earth.

ALL: AMEN

Leader: May God bless us with love
to bring forth new life.

ALL: AMEN

Leader: In the name of God, the maker of the whole world,
of Jesus, our new covenant,
and of the Holy Spirit, who opens eyes and hearts.

ALL: AMEN

Leader: Go in peace and be witnesses to hope.

ALL: THANKS BE TO GOD

From *Building a New World* (Canadian Catholic Organisation for Development and Peace, 1991)

Thus says the Lord who created you:
Do not be afraid, for I have redeemed you;
I have called you by your name, you are mine.
Should you pass through the sea, I will be with you;
or through rivers, they will not swallow you up.
Should you walk through fire, you will not be scorched
and the flames will not burn you.
For I am the Lord, your God, the Holy One of Israel, your saviour.

Isaiah 43:1-3

CHRISTIAN AID/ELAINE DUIGENAN

■ **Christian Aid supporters from Taunton get down to some serious fun and games promoting clean water issues**

17 See for yourself?

One of the best ways of finding out more about life in other countries is, of course, by visiting them. This chapter looks at 3 ways of doing this and offers practical hints on how to ensure that you, and the place you go to, get the most out of the visit.

FACTS ABOUT TOURISM:

- **Tourism is the world's biggest industry.**
- **Over 112 million people worldwide work in tourism – one in every 15 people with jobs on the planet.**
- **Twenty per cent of the world's tourists are under 25.**

But what are the effects of this massive industry on world development?

Brainstorm:
Tourism and the poor

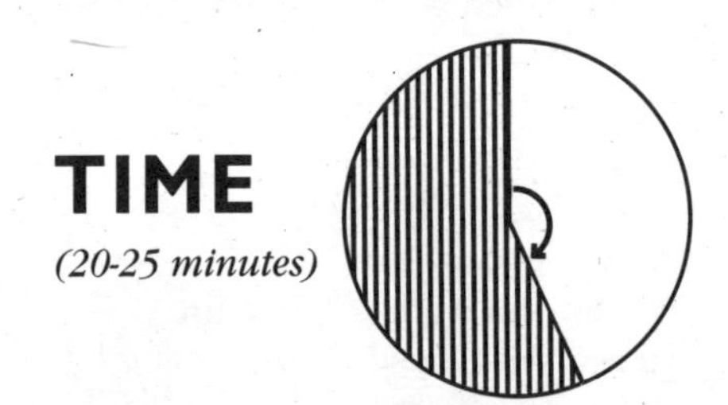

— Ask the group to shout out as many answers as they can to the following questions:

- **More and more people in the West are choosing to take their holidays in the Third World. Why do you think this is?**

(Possible answers include: a desire to go somewhere 'different'; the quest for the exotic; Third World countries tend to be cheap by western standards; people have seen these places on TV; they want to see how things really are; oh, and Third World countries tend to be sunny too!)

AUSTRALIAN CATHOLIC RELIEF

- **What are the advantages of tourism for Third World countries?**

(Possible answers include: tourism brings in money - especially hard currency like dollars which are needed for debt repayment and imports; it creates employment; it's an incentive to improve the roads and transport systems; it raises the profile of the country abroad.)

■ **What are the disadvantages?**

(Possible answers include: overcrowding; litter; wrecking the countryside; seeing so many people richer than themselves causes frustration for local people; disruption of wildlife; tourists take local plant/animal species home as souvenirs; pesticides and fertilisers used on recreational land, such as golf courses, affect the local water and soil; the jobs created tend to be servile and seasonal; raw sewage from tourist areas is often poured into the sea - a health hazard; tourists have priority in allocation of resources - unlimited clean water in hotels often means shortages elsewhere; tourists rarely see anything of the lives of ordinary people - misunderstanding is increased not reduced; sex tourism, common in some Third World countries, exploits the poverty of local women and children.)

POINTS FOR DISCUSSION

■ **Did the group find it easier to think of advantages or disadvantages? Why was this?**

— Read out the possible answers that the group didn't get. Are they surprised by any of them?

■ **Which of the advantages and disadvantages of tourism in the Third World also apply to tourism in the West? (The UK, for example, has around 17 million tourists a year.)**

■ **(If the group lives in a tourist area) What is your experience of tourists? (For all groups) How do you think you would view tourists if you were living in poverty in a 'tourist paradise'?**

A charter for Tourists

— Give out some brochures for holidays in Third World countries from a local travel agent. Ask the group in 3s and 4s to discuss the questions below and then meet back in the big group to compare answers (allow 20 minutes).

TIME
(45 minutes)

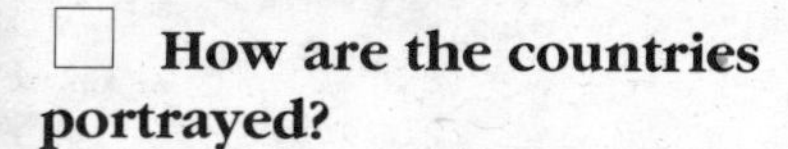

☐ **How are the countries portrayed?**

☐ **How true a picture is this?**

☐ **Why are they portrayed in this way?**

☐ **Are the people who live there mentioned? If so, how? If not, why not?**

☐ **How would you feel about the brochure if you were a poor person living in the country concerned?**

☐ **Imagine you are hosting a visit to the UK by a group of young people from another continent. Where would you take them? Would you try to give them a balanced picture of life here? If so, how? What wouldn't you show them? Why not?**

holiday brochures
papers and pens
poster-size version of 'The Charter for Tourists'

continued over page

— Split the group into pairs.

— Ask the pairs to imagine they are poor and living in a Third World 'tourist paradise'. They have been asked to write a 'Charter for Good Tourism'. (Allow 10-15 minutes).

— Back in the big group hear the charters.

— Display the poster-size version of the 'Charter for Tourists' below. How do the group's charters compare?

— Discuss the similarities and differences. What is the group's reaction to the 'real' charter? Are they surprised by anything in/not in it? Is the charter fair or is it too anti-western?

CHARTER FOR TOURISTS

STEVE BELL

God! How divinely Third World!

Prepared by a group of Asian Christians.

▲ Travel in a spirit of humility and with a genuine desire to learn more about the people of your host country. Be aware of the feelings of other people, thus preventing what might be offensive behaviour on your part. This applies very much to photography.

▲ Cultivate the habit of listening and observing, rather than merely hearing and seeing.

▲ Realise that the people in the country you are visiting have time concepts and habits different from your own. This does not make them inferior, only different.

▲ Instead of looking for that 'beach paradise', discover the enrichment of seeing a different way of life through other eyes.

▲ Acquaint yourself with local customs. What is courteous in one country may be quite the reverse in another - people will be happy to help you. This principle also applies to dress codes. Ways of dressing (particularly by women) which are quite acceptable in Europe can cause deep offence overseas.

▲ Instead of the western practice of 'knowing all the answers', cultivate the habit of asking questions.

▲ Remember that you are only one of thousands of tourists visiting this country and do not expect special privileges.

▲ When you are shopping, remember that the 'bargain' you obtained was possible only because of the low wages paid to the maker.

▲ Do not make promises to people in your host country unless you can carry them through.

▲ Spend time reflecting on your daily experiences in an attempt to deepen your understanding. It has been said that "what enriches you, may rob and violate others."

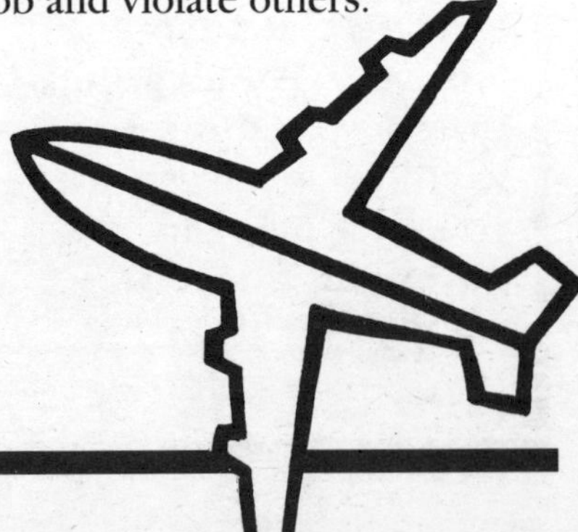

FOLLOW UP

1 *Show the video 'Jamaica: No Problem'. It makes a number of points about the benefits and dangers of Jamaica's tourist industry. It lasts 20 minutes and comes with its own discussion material.*

2 Join Tourism Concern. This is a network of people concerned, and taking action, about the impact of tourism on host communities It can provide advice, a handbook and information on how to be a sensitive tourist (see Addresses Section at the back).

2 WORKING ABROAD AS A VOLUNTEER

This is an area where, even more than usual, good intentions are not enough. Most agencies sending volunteers overseas now require a minimum of 2 years and are usually looking for people with professional qualifications. Moreover, it is very important that potential volunteers have thought carefully about all the implications.

Questions to ask yourself:

- **What do I expect to get out of volunteering? Where do these expectations come from?**
- **How much time do I have? Why do I want to go to the Third World? Why not be a volunteer in the UK?**
- **What are my attitudes to the Third World? Where have these attitudes come from? Am I willing for these to change? Am I willing for my whole outlook on life to change?**

If you can answer these questions satisfactorily, the next thing to do is to consult the following directories of volunteering opportunities (available from good bookshops or direct from the publishers - see Addresses Section at the back):

Volunteer Work (£7.99). Published by Central Bureau for Educational Visits and Exchanges.

The International Directory of Voluntary Work (£8.95). Edited by David Woodworth and published by Vacation Work.

Volunteering and Overseas Development: a guide to opportunities (50p) Compiled by Returned Volunteer Action.

3 YOUTH EXCHANGES

a) Why have youth exchanges?

Youth exchanges are not holidays. They are a source of education not only for the participants, but also for their families and the churches or other organisations which send and receive them. The aims of a real exchange are:

- To expose the participants, hosts and guests, to one another so that a process of mutual learning and appreciation can take place.
- To forge permanent links between people of different cultures.

b) What is involved in organising an exchange?

You will need to start your thinking and planning in good time (18 months to 2 years before the first leg of the exchange) as an enormous amount of work is necessary.

Consider:

- How you are going to make contact with a suitable partner group. Contacts may be made through your minister/priest or through friends with overseas links.

■ Aims and expectations on both sides.

■ The numbers in each party. It is difficult to prevent large groups from becoming 'tour parties'. Six people plus a leader is probably the ideal.

■ How much money you can raise. Your partner group may need a lot of help with travel and other costs. You will therefore probably have to raise funds for both outgoing and incoming visits.

■ Budgets, dates, visas and other official requirements, health precautions and briefings.

For help with organising exchanges contact one of the following (see Adresses Section at the back):

Commonwealth Youth Exchange Council
Youth Exchange Centre
Christians Abroad

"Tourism is another kind of slavery for Dominicans. Spaniards call tourism 'pueria' – whoring – and that's what it is, pleasing foreigners. It's corrupting like pollution. Take our region, Samanà. If the government gave Samanà a million dollars for agricultural projects, we could be exporting fruit and vegetables and living well. We could have solar energy and irrigation systems. Instead, they talk of a golf course. Can you imagine what an insult it is to us who have always lived from the land, to put down a golf course among us?"

A farmer in the Dominican Republic talking with Alistair Reid, *The New Yorker*, February 24, 1992

"Tourism has brought no benefits to us, only to the rich . . . It only brings us problems as we had to move . . . The tourists own Acapulco."

Woman from Acapulco, Mexico talking to Liam Kane, Oxfam education worker

AUSTRALIAN CATHOLIC RELIEF

TOURIST/HOME MOVIES

"And here's one of an Indian
Selling Ralph a trinket -
I suppose he'll use the money
To buy some wine and drink it."

Tourist, do you also
Tour the Black Man's slums
Photographing winos,
Photographing bums?
Do you really think you're welcome,
Do you really think it's funny
The things that starving people do
For little bits of money?
Do you see the anger?
Do you see the pain?
That says in silence "Go away
And don't come back again."

Bob Bacon, a native American c. 1980

The British tourist is always happy abroad so long as the natives are waiters.

Robert Morely, actor, 1958

18 Acting up *or* Luvvies for Justice

The following 2 sketches could be performed in church services, during the kind of evening described in Chapter Sixteen, or anywhere else the group wants to make its point dramatically. Feel free to photocopy these sketches – for performances only!

1 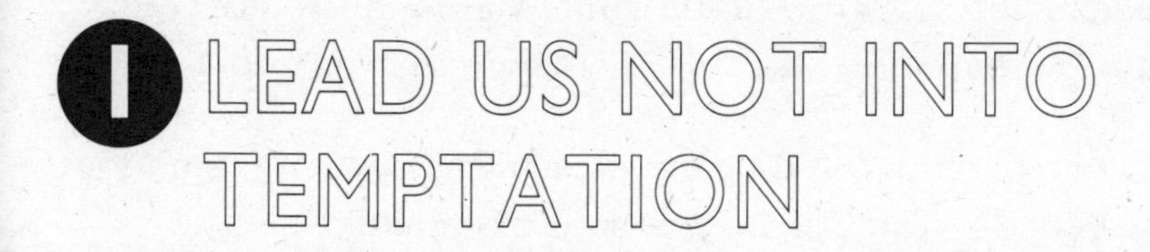

A sketch for 3 people. The only prop strictly necessary is a Bible. However, as the costumes for the devils should be as obvious, spectacular and over-the-top as possible, you might also have the group make 2 tridents.

*Thunder and lightning (**do your best!**). Enter 2 devils - from opposite sides.*

Mephistopheles (Meph) is cheerful looking, perhaps whistling. Screw-top is clearly depressed.

MEPH: **What's the matter with you then son? Come on, cheer up, eh? It may never happen.**

SCREW TOP: **Too late, I'm afraid. It already has. Oh, what a mess my afterlife is. (*On brink of tears*)**

MEPH: **For Satan's sake, man, get a grip on yourself. What's happened?**

SCREW TOP: **Well, I've just had my 6-monthly appraisal with The Boss and er . . . well, suffice it to say I haven't exactly been meeting my performance targets. He gave me a real roasting I can tell you. (*Feels bottom tenderly*)**

MEPH: **Now come on er . . . what's your name?**

SCREW TOP: **Screw-top. Yours?**

MEPH: **Mephistopheles, at your service. (*Bows*)**

SCREW TOP: **Mephistopheles! The Mephistopheles? The guy they call the 'Faust Operator'. (*To audience*) It's a literary joke. Never mind. (*To Meph*) You're a real legend, you know that?**

MEPH: **(*With obvious mock modesty*) I believe I do have a certain reputation for success, yes. Mind you, I'm not one for resting on my laurels.**

SCREW TOP: **Why, what have you been up to lately?**

MEPH: **Well, let's just say Nintendo Game-Boys didn't get so popular on their own. (*Note: Insert any topical references of your own here*)**

SCREW TOP: **Blimey! That was you. Amazing. Look Mephistopheles, I don't suppose . . . no . . . why should you? A great devil like you and a, a . . . total loser like me . . . (*About to cry again*)**

MEPH: **You want a few tips? It'd be my pleasure. Now why don't you tell me exactly what The Boss is so cross about?**

SCREW TOP: **Gosh, thanks, Mephistopheles. Well, it's the Christians in my patch . . .**

MEPH: **(*Witheringly*) Oh them. (*Wearily*) What have they been up to this time?**

SCREW TOP: **Well, they've started really taking seriously all that stuff about caring for the world, bringing Good News to the poor, building the Enemy's kingdom, you know.**

MEPH: **And it's not just lip service?**

SCREW TOP: **'Fraid not. I hoped desperately that it was for a while, but this lot really mean it.**

MEPH: **I see. Yes, that is serious. And you've tried all the usual things on them – concern for the Third World was an '80s thing; the poor are beyond help . . .**

TOGETHER: **Charity begins at home; it's sad but there's nothing we can do.**

SCREW TOP: **Yep. I've done all that.**

MEPH: **And it had no effect?**

SCREW TOP: **None at all.**

MEPH: **Hmm. Let me think . . . (*Pause*) Got it! I think this calls for the 'Real World Ruse'. (*Smugly*) Temptation number 543a in the manual, I think you'll find.**

SCREW TOP: **Gosh, Mephistopheles, you really know your stuff eh? So how does this er . . . 'Real World Ruse' thing work?**

MEPH: **Beautifully, in my experience. And it's so simple too. All you have to do is get the (*contemptuously*) 'concerned person' to pretend that his or her little life is 'the real world' and therefore that it's irresponsible dreaming to worry about anything else. Even better, use the same phrase, 'the real world' to describe the most brutal way of arranging life you can imagine. Your subjects will be saying: "It's tough out there"; "We don't owe each other a living" and so on – all the phrases The Boss loves – in no time. You follow me?**

SCREW TOP: **Er . . . I think so.**

MEPH: **Are you sure?**

SCREW TOP: **Well, it's just that it seems so ridiculous. People really fall for this do they?**

MEPH: **Of course they do. Remember what happened during Christmas 1914.**

SCREW TOP: **Ah, I see what you mean. (*Pause*) Er . . .what did happen in Christmas 1914?**

MEPH: **Tut! What do they teach you young devils these days? (*Pompously*) Christmas 1914 was perhaps the finest ever use of the 'Real World Ruse', historically speaking. I mean, there were the soldiers of both sides, playing football and chatting away in no-man's-land – until, that is, we managed to convince the generals that that sort of behaviour was irresponsible dreaming, whereas the same people shooting each other by the thousand was the 'real world'. The men were soon back in the trenches then, I can tell you.**

SCREW TOP: **Fair enough. But I still can't imagine Christians falling for the 'Ruse'.**

MEPH: **Oh but they do, I can assure you. Let me loose on a Christian determined to change the world today, and I'll show you someone worrying only about whether his carpets go with his curtains tomorrow. After all, carpets are part of the 'real world' thing and hungry people thousands of miles away are not – or so it's easy to convince them. It never fails. Anyway, enough talk. What I really need is one of those Christians of yours to demonstrate what I mean.**

SCREW TOP: **(*Looking into the wings, then with obvious theatricality*) Oh! Look! Here comes one now.**

TOGETHER: **(*Turning to face audience; stagily*) What a stroke of luck.**

Enter Christian, carrying Bible.

CHRISTIAN: **(*Thinking aloud*) That really was a most moving service, I must say. That's it, now. I've talked about it long enough. The time has come for action. I'm going straight down to the CAFOD/Christian Aid/SCIAF office (*whichever is appropriate*) to see what I can do to help. And I'm going to find out more about the world, and I'm going to start being far more generous with my time and money and I'm . . .**

SCREW TOP: **See what I mean? It's hopeless.**

MEPH: **Piece of cake. Watch this.**

Meph goes up to Christian and whispers at length in his ear. Screw-top looks on tensely with his fingers crossed.

CHRISTIAN: **(*Thinking aloud as before*) That's true, mind you. Where will it all end? I mean, I can't go changing my entire life at my age. There's the family to consider for a start and the mortgage. It's such a lovely house, I wouldn't want anything to happen there, just as we've got the sitting room right at last. Well, sort of – I'm still not sure that the carpet matches the curtains . . .**

Meph looks significantly and triumphantly at Screw-top. Christian begins to exit.

CHRISTIAN: **(*As he goes*) I mean we don't owe each other a living . . . you've got to live in the real world after all . . .**

Exit

MEPH: **(*Bowing theatrically to Screw-top*) And that's all there is to it.**

SCREW TOP: **(*Lost in admiration*) Mephistopheles, you're an absolute genius! I've never seen anything like it in my eternal life. It's really that easy? (*Little chuckle*) S/he really fell for it didn't s/he? Number 543a . . .**

MEPH: **So why don't you have a go?**

SCREW TOP: **Can't wait. Just show me some Christians and I'll be in there.**

MEPH: **(*Indicating congregation*) Well, there's some.**

SCREW TOP: **(*Theatrical double-take*) Good Satan. So there are. (*Tone of farewell*) Right then, here I go. Wish me luck.**

Cast take their bows.

THE END

2 THE PRICE IS RIGHT: A NEW LOOK AT LUKE

(Based, loosely, on Luke 16-19 where 3 people respond to the same choices in very different ways.)

A sketch for 4 people. Despite appearances, the characters do not all need to be played by males.

The 'set' is very simple: a table at each side, one behind which the 3 contestants need to stand and be seen; the other with the 2 items covered by cloths. Luke should stand centrally.

Props required: 2 tables; 3 small cards for Luke; bank bag (stuffed and with money poking out of the top); CAFOD/Christian Aid/SCIAF poster and collecting tin; 2 cloths; copy of 'The Good News according to Luke' (or, failing that, the Bible).

More ambitious groups could make cue cards saying CHEER, CLAP, BOO! Decide if these are likely to embarrass the congregation/audience and, if not, get someone to hold them up at the appropriate times to encourage audience response. The appropriate times should be clear enough from the script. If you don't use the cards, group members not in the cast should sit at the front, play the audience and make the noises required.

Costume tips are in the text itself.

Enter St Luke in a showbiz, game-show way, encouraging audience applause. He should be wearing a jacket and tie.

LUKE: **Hello, ladies and gentlemen and welcome to 'The Price is Right'. My name's St Luke and, as usual, I'll be asking some lucky contestants to come on down, join me here and try and guess the value of certain objects. (*Indicates cloth-covered objects*) So, without further ado, (*Looks at card and then says loudly*) Dives, COME ON DOWN!**

Enter Dives, arms aloft, from audience/congregation. Goes behind table. He should be dressed as sumptuously as possible, preferably in purple.

LUKE: **Hello, Dives, mate. Nervous?**

DIVES: **A little, Luke, yes.**

LUKE: **There's no need, mate. We're all right behind you. (*Reading card*) I see from your card here that you're a 'wealth creator'** by trade and that your hobbies include feasting magnificently every day.

AUDIENCE	*Wooooooo!!!!*
DIVES:	**Well, I do regard myself as something of a foodie, yes.**
LUKE:	**OK. So, just relax Dives, enjoy the show and, of course if you win tonight's star prize, you could be feasting even more magnificently in future. (*Faces audience again and glances at next card*) Now then, Richard Youngman, COME ON DOWN!**
	Enter rich young man, arms aloft, from congregation/audience. Goes behind table.
LUKE:	**So, Mr Youngman – or can I call you Richard?**
RICH:	**Actually all my friends call me Rich.**
LUKE:	**OK. Rich Youngman it is. (*To audience*) Clever stuff eh? (*Reads card*) And you're a member of one of our wealthiest families. (*To audience*) As you can see, this is a class show, ladies and gentlemen. (*To Rich*) Now, Rich, I hear you have an unusual achievement to tell us about . . . ?**
RICH:	**(*Mock modesty*) Oh . . . yes . . . I know what you mean. Well, er . . . I don't like to talk about it but I've er . . . kept the commandments from my earliest days.**
LUKE:	**(*Encourages audience applause*) And there's not many of us can say that, eh, ladies and gentlemen? (*Perhaps with a significant look at the vicar/priest/minister. Then glances at next card*) And, finally, then, Zaccheus, COME ON DOWN!**
	Enter Zaccheus from audience/congregation, less triumphantly than the other 2. Ideally, he should be played by someone walking on their knees, wearing a long coat. He goes behind the table, which he just peers over.
LUKE:	**(*Reading card*) Well, Zacc, I see from your card that you're a tax collector (*Encourages audience boos, then cuts them*) No, come on ladies and gentlemen, seriously, where would we be without our friends from the Inland Revenue? A lot richer, I suppose – though not as rich as they are. (*Little laugh*) God bless you Zacc, only joking. You just relax and enjoy yourself. Don't worry at all. Oh, sorry, I didn't mean to say 'tall'. (*Little laugh*)**
	(*To all 3*) So, welcome everybody. I'm sure you know the rules. I show you various items, you guess what they're worth and the nearest guess to the real value wins. What could be

simpler? Just remember that my decision is final. Ready? (*They all murmur 'Yes.'*)

And the first item is (*pulls cloth from first item to reveal the stuffed bank bag*) wealth and the social status that goes with it. Dives?

DIVES: **I think that's worth everything. How else can you afford clothes, good food, wine – all the little things that make life bearable.**

LUKE: **OK. Rich?**

RICH: **Well, it makes me sad to say this, but I'm afraid I agree with Dives. I'll say it's worth everything too – but I'm still a nice guy who keeps all the commandments. Or have I mentioned that already?**

LUKE: **I think you might have done. Zacc?**

ZACCHEUS: **I used to agree with these two, but, you know, I'm not sure I do any more. In fact, I don't think wealth is worth what I've always paid for it. I think I'm going to give half mine away, and if I've swindled anybody, I'll pay them back fourfold.**

LUKE: **Interesting answer – and Zaccheus is absolutely right. (*Encourages audience applause*) Rather surprisingly, tonight's star prize could be his – if he gets just one more correct answer.**

So, let's have the next item. And it's (*pulls cloth from second item to reveal the CAFOD/ Christian Aid/SCIAF poster and collecting tin*) genuine concern for the poor. Dives, think carefully now. You need this one, mate. What value do you place on genuine concern for the poor?

DIVES: **I know this. It's a trick question isn't it? There are no poor people any more – at least none that I've ever noticed. In any case, charity must begin at home, and I'd do anything for my brothers.**

LUKE: **Uh-huh. Rich?**

RICH: **I couldn't disagree more. We must have enormous concern for the poor – it says so in the scriptures, which, of course, I do happen to know rather well.**

LUKE: **So, how much would you actually be prepared to give?**

RICH: **Ah . . . you mean me personally?**

LUKE: **Yes.**

RICH: **Well, me personally . . . er . . . well, a quid every now and then? Max. You see, I'm a man of great wealth. There's no point just giving it away. I prefer to use my money to er . . . benefit the community, by er . . . keeping it all for myself.**

LUKE: **I see. What about you then Zacc?**

ZACCHEUS: **Well, again, I've recently changed my ideas on this one. I'd say concern for the poor is worth a great deal. I'd pay a lot for it. Most of my personal and financial security in fact.**

LUKE: **And, once again, Zaccheus is absolutely right! (*Encourages applause*) And, yes, he is indeed the shock winner of tonight's star prize which is salvation coming upon his house – oh, and a pair of platform shoes. (*Encourages applause, which Zaccheus acknowledges*)**

And so we say goodbye to Rich . . . (*Rich exits with theatrical sadness*) who er . . . goes away sad. And also to Dives. (*Exit Dives*) Give our love to everyone in Hades, mate.

(*To audience*) And that's all we've got time for, ladies and gentlemen. Once more, the old clock on the wall has caught up with us. But remember you can always play the game at home, by deciding what you think things are really worth. In fact, it's impossible not to. And don't forget that if you need any tips on the answers, my book of the series is now available from all good-book shops. (*Holds up 'Good News according to Luke' – or Bible*)

Goodnight and congratulations again to this week's winner, Zaccheus. (*Zaccheus comes out from behind table and joins Luke in the middle. Both wave as audience applaud.*)

Cast take their bows.

THE END

Groups now bitten by the acting bug should try and get hold of one of the booklets in the *'Eh Jesus? Yes Peter'* series from the Iona Community (Wild Goose Publications; see Addresses Section). It's full of good, funny religious sketches.

19 Let us Pray

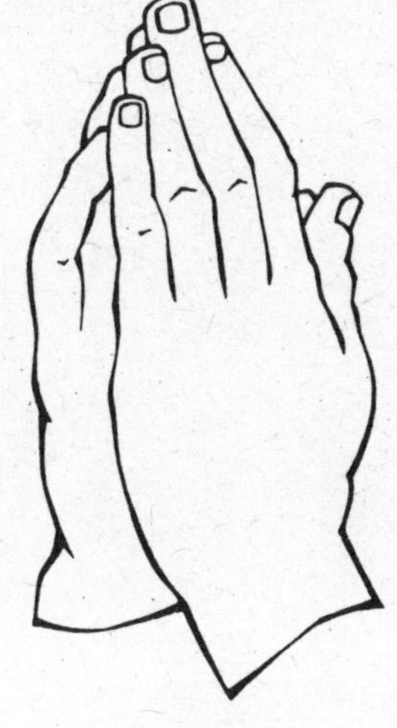

There is plenty of worship material throughout this book – meditations in Chapters Eight and Ten, for example, and the reflections at the end of each chapter which can always be the basis of a time of prayer on that chapter's issues.
This chapter provides some general worship ideas. Obviously, different groups will be comfortable with different sorts of prayer – so do adapt the following ideas for your group.

A THE CROSS OF LIFE

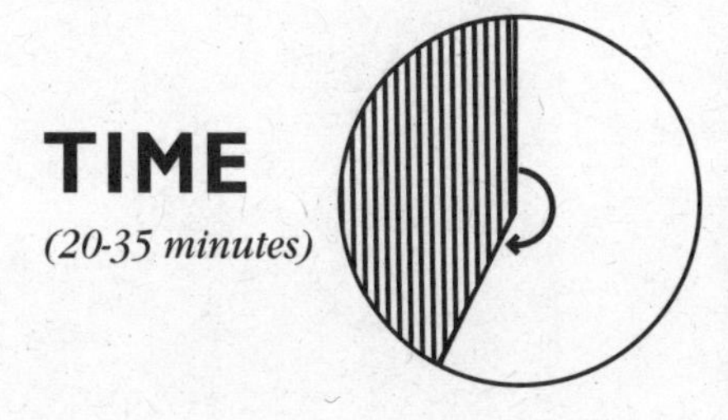

wood and nails to make a cross
paints and paint brushes

This is not, strictly speaking, an idea for worship, but a 'prop' for group prayer.

— Show the group the El Salvador Cross and describe the story of Maria Cristina Gomez:

> *During the 1980s, civil war claimed the lives of 70,000 people in El Salvador. If the victim was a member of a Christian community, the members would commemorate them by making a simple wooden cross and decorating it with pictures symbolic of their life and concerns.*
>
> *The cross here was made in memory of Maria Cristina Gomez, - a primary school teacher and an active member of her local church. In April 1989, as Maria came out of school a van with darkened windows pulled up beside her. Her pupils watched as several armed men pulled her inside, kicking and screaming. Later, in another part of the city, the same van stopped at the edge of the road. The door slid open and her body was pushed out. There were acid burns on it, marks of beating on her face and four bullet wounds.*
>
> *The situation in El Salvador has now improved, but there are still many situations throughout the world where people live in fear for their lives.*

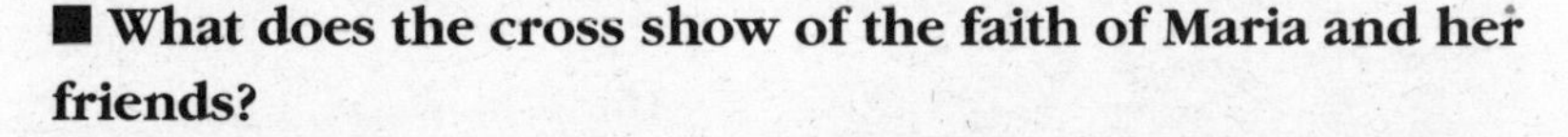

■ **What does the cross show of the faith of Maria and her friends?**

— Make a large cross showing the lives and concerns of your group. Once you have made the basic structure, ask every member to paint something representing themselves and the situations they want to offer to God. (Try to encourage the group to think about their wider, global concerns as well as their personal ones.)

— Whenever the group prays, use the cross as part of that prayer. Perhaps, too, you could get permission to display it in your church.

The Cross was a gift to the Codena de la Esperanza Maria Cristina Gomez from her family and Baptist Church, Shalom, El Salvador

Artist: Fernando Llort

B ACT OF DEDICATION

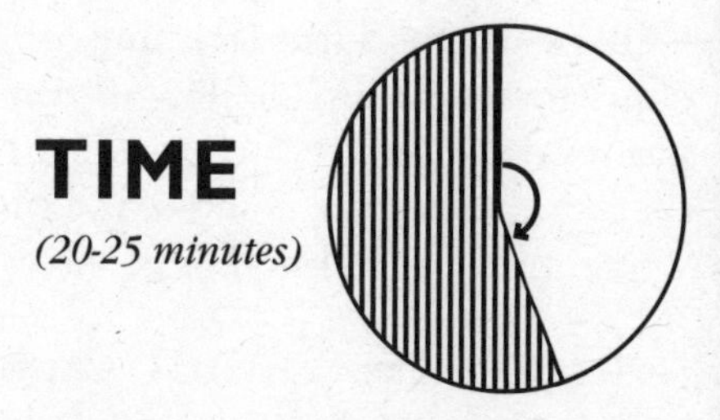

Use the following idea in a service of dedication with suitable prayers and hymns, where the group members offer what they can do for God and his world.

YOU WILL NEED
cross
papers and pens
copies of the hymns and choruses

— Explain to the group that in a brief time of silence people will have a chance to think about and write down one step they can take towards greater justice in the world and that these will then be put by the cross and offered to God.

Leader: ***Jesus' call to follow him into fullness of life is not an easy or comfortable one. Sometimes the thought of all that might be involved can paralyse us into doing nothing. But Jesus doesn't call us to perfection and then leave us to get on with it. His call is rather to advance with him a step at a time. Let us therefore take some time now to ask him in the silence of our hearts what might be the next step for each of us. If and when you feel you can, write down on the paper some resolution, however small, you feel able to make that will enable you to respond more authentically to God in your life.***

— Have a time of silence while people write down a resolution.

Leader: ***We will now collect up the resolutions and lay them at the foot of the cross as an offering to Jesus. We do this knowing that he will accept and bless our efforts to follow him.***

— Collect the papers and place them at the foot of the cross. Meanwhile everybody sings a hymn or chorus of offering.

— Alternatively, the papers can be attached to the cross whilst laid flat on the floor. It can then be raised during the following prayer.

PRAYER

Lord, we believe in you. Help us to demonstrate our faith in everything we do, so that together with your people all over the world and in your strength, we may give ourselves to build your kingdom. May our resolutions become reality and our whole lives reflect our willingness to follow you. We make our prayer through Christ our Lord.
Amen.

C PRAYER FOR THE WORLD

YOU WILL NEED
large map of the world
candles or night-lights (one per person)

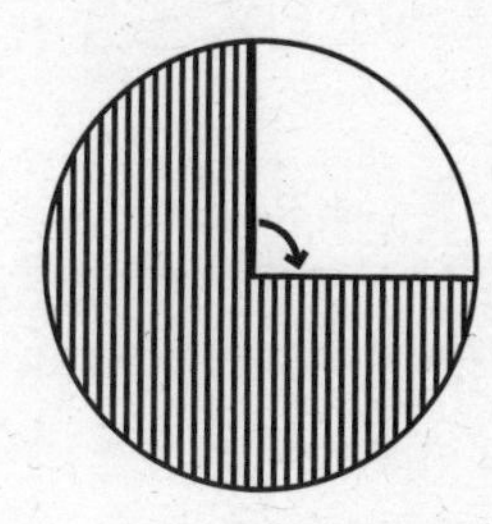

— Lay the map (the biggest you can find) on the ground. Seat everyone in a circle around it. Place candles around the map leaving gaps between them so that people can get at it.

— Explain that during the time of shared prayer, people are invited to come forward individually, take one of the candles and place it on a part of the world they'd particularly like to pray for. As they do so, they should say the name of the place and give a brief explanation why they want to pray for it.

— Teach the Taizé chant: "O Christe Domine Jesu." It's worth taking your time doing this as it is very powerful, sung properly in parts:

JAQUES BERTIERS (LES PRESSES DE TAIZE, FRANCE)

THE SERVICE

Begin with the chant.

READER 1: Psalm 34:3-6; 17-18.

ALL SING: O Christe Domine Jesu.

LEADER: Lord, we come before you, aware of all those parts of your world where people are suffering from lack of food, from exploitation or from war. We ask you now to be near those who mourn, all the poor who cry to you for help, and all the poor who do not. Listen to our prayers as we now bring their needs before you.

SHARED PRAYER: *Invite group members to place their candles on the map on those parts of the world they wish to remember before God. Judge when this time has come to an end and then say the following collect:*

LEADER: Lord, bless your world. May that day come, promised in Scripture, when you wipe the tears from every eye and all people live in the light of your kingdom. We make our prayer through Jesus Christ.

ALL: Amen.

ALL SING: O Christe, Domine Jesu.

The Lord's Prayer.

Final hymn or chorus of thanksgiving.

Lots of worship material can be supplied by CAFOD, Christian Aid and SCIAF on request. Full details in the Resources Section at the back of the book.

Other very useful sources of worship ideas are:

***Celebrating One World*, from CAFOD (£6:95)**

***Bread of Tomorrow*, from Christian Aid (£6:99)**

***Windows on Worship*, ed. Ron Ingamells (National Council of YMCAs)**

Anything by Wild Goose Publications, Iona Community.

WHAT TO LOOK FOR...?

USEFUL RESOURCES

CHAPTER 1

Rich Christians in an Age of Hunger
A book by Ronald J Sider for anybody interested in the issue of Christianity and money. Published by Hodder & Stoughton. (£3.99) Available at most Christian bookshops or from CAFOD.

CHAPTER 3

'Savithri'
A 15-minute video exploring the life of a young girl in south India. Available from Christian Aid. (Free hire)

'Bright Lights, Big Cities'
A section of the video 'Land, Hope and Glory?' which depicts the lives and hopes of street children in Brazil. Available from CAFOD youth office. (Free hire)

CHAPTER 4

'Africa: Our Own Story'
A 20-minute video looking at Africa through the eyes of Africans. Available from Christian Aid. (Free hire)

CHAPTER 6

'Trading Game'
Simulation game for 15-30 players aged 9-plus to help players understand how trade affects national prosperity. Playing time 90 minutes. Available from Christian Aid. (50p)

'Trading Trainers'
Simulation game for 15-36 players aged 13-plus. It shows how the makers of trainers in Latin America suffer from unjust trading conditions. Playing time 80 minutes. Available from CAFOD.

'Market Trading'
Simulation game for 15-30 players aged 14-plus to help players understand the impact of the European Single Market and trade restrictions on the world's poorest countries. Playing time 80 minutes. Available from Christian Aid. (£1)

'Trade for Change'
A set of 20 slides with commentary on the major issues of trading injustice. Available from Christian Aid. (£5)

'Bitter Sweet'
A 20-minute video showing the effect of international trade on sugar workers in the Dominican Republic. Available from Christian Aid. (Free hire)

New Consumer
Regular information about consumerism. Address shown in next section.

Shopping for a Better World
A handy book which evaluates 2,500 major brands by various ethical criteria. Available from New Consumer. (£4.99)

CHAPTER 7

'Deals for Destruction'
A 30-minute video which may be too complex for some younger groups. Available from Campaign Against the Arms Trade. (Hire £10)

CHAPTER 8

We Left Because We Had To
A book aimed at young people, full of information, ideas for action and personal stories about refugees. Available from the Refugee Council or CAFOD. (£5) Videos also available. (Free hire)

CHAPTER 9

'Same Rights for Severina'
A 30-minute video which explores human rights in Brazil, and demonstrates how democracy does not necessarily guarantee such rights. Available from Christian Aid. (Free hire)

CHAPTER 10

'Women Hold up Half the Sky'
A resource pack for use with children aged 11-14 looking at the Christian dimension of women in tackling development. Available from CAFOD, Christian Aid and SCIAF. (£3)

'Manomiya'
Board game for 5-10 players to raise awareness about women in development. Playing time 80 minutes. Available from Returned Volunteer Action. (£8)

'AIDS and Development'
An information pack on AIDS in the Third World. Available from CAFOD. (£1.95)

CHAPTER 11

'A Matter of Interest'
A 13-minute video cartoon explaining simply the origins and effects of the debt crisis. Available from Christian Aid. (Free hire)

'Jamaica: No Problem'
A 20-minute video showing the effect of the island's massive debt on Jamaican life. Available from Christian Aid. (Free hire)

'Hell to Pay'
A 15-minute extract from the video compilation 'Land, Hope and Glory?' in which Bolivian women talk about the effects of debt on their lives. Available from CAFOD youth office. (Free hire)

CHAPTER 12

'TIMBER!'
Simulation game for 25-40 people exploring the conflicting uses of the rainforest. Available CAFOD. (£1.50)

'Renewing the Earth: Youth Guide'
A resource pack for youth groups interested in exploring the links between development and the environment. Available from CAFOD. (£3)

CHAPTER 13

'Yonder Peasant'
A 22-minute cartoon videostrip exploring the Christian response to world poverty, through a fantasy parable. Available from Christian Aid. (Free hire)

'Faith and Struggle in Central America'
A resource pack for young people aged 16-18 exploring faith and action, and the basic concepts of liberation theology. Available from Christian Aid and CAFOD. (£3)

CHAPTER 15

The Food Guide
Recipes from around the world can be found in this exciting book. Available from New Internationalist. (£9:99)

Bread of Tomorrow
A book of prayers and meditations for every occasion. Available from Christian Aid. (£6:99)

Celebrating One World
A book containing prayers from around the world. Available from CAFOD. (£6:95)

'The Tiger and the Oxen'
A 28-minute video providing a good introduction to some of the issues of rural development in India. Available from Christian Aid. (Free hire)

'Paper Bag Game'
Simulation game for 10-35 players aged 9-plus. It gives participants a powerful sense of what it's like to be locked in the struggle for survival in Calcutta. Playing time 45 minutes. Available from Christian Aid. (50p)

'Same Rights for Severina'
A 26-minute video exploring the effects of poverty in Brazil and what people are doing to overcome them. Available from Christian Aid. (Free hire)

'VIVA!'
A resource pack for young people focusing on Latin America. Available from CAFOD. (£4.50)

'Working in Partnership with Brazil'
Free pack including prayers and recipes from Brazil, available from CAFOD. Other packs available on Kenya, Sudan, Ethiopia/Eritrea and South Africa.

CHAPTER 16

Free leaflets with lots of fundraising hints and suggestions are available on request from CAFOD, Christian Aid and SCIAF.

CHAPTER 19

'Holy Ground'
A booklet of Bible studies for young people tackling questions of poverty, suffering and lifestyles. Available from Christian Aid. (£1.50)

CAFOD, Christian Aid, and SCIAF also have a wide range of worship materials including slide meditations, prayers from around the world, Bible studies and specific ideas for CAFOD Fast days, Christian Aid Week, and SCIAF Sunday – available on request.

USEFUL ADDRESSES

AMNESTY INTERNATIONAL
99-119 Roseberry Avenue, London, EC1R 4RE
Tel: 071-278 6000

ANTI-APARTHEID MOVEMENT
13 Mandela Street, London, NW1 0DW
Tel: 071-387 7966

BABY MILK ACTION COALITION
23 St Andrew's Street, Cambridge, CB2 3AX
Tel: 0223-464420

BAPTIST UNION
PO Box 44, Baptist House, 129 The Broadway, Didcot, Oxon, OX11 8RT
Tel: 0235-512077

COUNCIL OF CHURCHES FOR BRITAIN AND IRELAND (CCBI)
Interchurch House, 35-41 Lower Marsh, Waterloo, London, SE1 7RG
Tel: 071-620 4444

CAMPAIGN AGAINST THE ARMS TRADE
11 Goodwin Street, London, N4 3HQ
Tel: 071-281 0297

CAMPAIGN FOR NUCLEAR DISARMAMENT
162 Holloway Rd, London, N7 8DQ
Tel: 071-700 2393

CAFOD
2 Romero Close, Stockwell Road, London, SW9 9TY
Tel: 071-733 7900

CATHOLIC YOUTH SERVICE
39 Fitzjohns Avenue, London, NW3 5JT
Tel: 071-435 3596

CENTRAL AMERICAN HUMAN RIGHTS COMMITTEE
83 Margaret Street, London, W1N 7HB
Tel: 071-631 4200

CENTRAL BUREAU FOR EDUCATIONAL VISITS AND EXCHANGES
Seymour Mews House, Seymour Mews, London, W1H 9PE
Tel: 071-486 5101

CENTRE FOR GLOBAL EDUCATION
University of York, York, YO1 5DD
Tel: 0904-433444

CENTRE FOR WORLD DEVELOPMENT EDUCATION (CWDE)
1 Catton Street, London, W1R 4AB
Tel: 071-831 3844

CHRISTIANS ABROAD
1 Stockwell Green, London SW9 9JF
Tel : 071-737 7811

CHRISTIAN AID
PO Box 100, London, SE1 7RT
Tel: 071-620 4444
PO Box 21, Cardiff, CF4 2DL
PO Box 11, Edinburgh, EH11 1EL

CHURCH OF ENGLAND, GENERAL SYNOD BOARD OF EDUCATION
Church House, Great Smith Street, London, SW1P 3BL
Tel: 071-222 9011

CHURCH OF SCOTLAND DEPARTMENT OF EDUCATION
121 George Street, Edinburgh, EH2 4YN
Tel: 031-225 5722

CHURCH MISSIONARY SOCIETY (CMS)
157 Waterloo Road, London, SE1 8UU
Tel: 071-928 8681

COMMONWEALTH INSTITUTE
Kensington High Street, London, W8 6NQ
Tel: 071-603 4535

COMMONWEALTH YOUTH EXCHANGE COUNCIL
7 Lion Yard, Tremadoc Road, London, SW4 7NF
Tel: 071-498 6151

COUNCIL FOR ENVIRONMENTAL EDUCATION
University of Reading, London Road, Reading, RG1 5AQ
Tel: 0734-756 061

DEVELOPMENT EDUCATION ASSOCIATION (DEA)
6 Endsleigh Street, London, WC1H 0DS
Tel: 071-388 2670

FARMERS' WORLD NETWORK
Arthur Rank Centre, National Agricultural Centre, Stonleigh, Kenilworth, Warks, CV8 2LZ
Tel: 0203 696969

FELLOWSHIP OF RECONCILIATION
40-46 Harleyford Road, Vauxhall, London, SE11 5AY
Tel: 071-582 9054

FRIENDS OF THE EARTH AND EARTH ACTION (YOUTH SECTION)
26-28 Underwood Street, London, N1 7JQ
Tel: 071-490 1555

FRONTIER YOUTH TRUST
Scripture Union House, 130 City Road, London, EC1V 2NJ
Tel: 071-250 1966

GREENPEACE
Cannonbury Villas, London, N1 2PN
Tel: 071-354 5100

INTERNATIONAL BROADCASTING TRUST (IBT)
2 Ferdinand Place, London, NW1 8EE
Tel: 071-482 2847

INTERNATIONAL DEFENCE AND AID FUND FOR SOUTHERN AFRICA
Canon Collins House, 64 Essex Road, London, N1 8LR
Tel: 071-359 9181

INTERMEDIATE TECHNOLOGY DEVELOPMENT GROUP (ITDG)
Myson House, Railway Terrace, Rugby, CV21 3HT
Tel: 0788-560 631

IONA COMMUNITY (WILD GOOSE PUBLICATIONS)
Community House, Pearce Institute, 840 Govan Road, Glasgow, G51 3UU
Tel: 041-445 4561

METHODIST ASSOCIATION OF YOUTH CLUBS
2 Chester House, Pages Lane, Muswell Hill, London, N10 1PR
Tel: 081-444 9845

MINORITY RIGHTS GROUP (MRG)
379 Brixton Road, London, SW9 7DE
Tel: 071-978 9498

NEW CONSUMER
52 Elswick Rd, Newcastle-Upon-Tyne, NE4 6JH
Tel: 091-272 1148

NEW INTERNATIONALIST PUBLICATIONS LTD
55 Rectory Road, Oxford, OX4 1BW
Tel: 0865-728181

NICARAGUA SOLIDARITY CAMPAIGN
c/o Red Rose Club, 129 Seven Sisters Rd, London, N7 7QG
Tel: 071-272 9619

ONE WORLD WEEK
PO Box 100, London, SE1 7RT
Tel: 071-620 4444

OXFAM
274 Banbury Road, Oxford, OX2 7DZ
Tel: 0865-311311

PAX CHRISTI
9 Henry Road, London, N4 2LH
Tel: 081-800 4612

PHILIPPINES RESOURCE CENTRE
74-78 Long Lane, London, SE1 4AV
Tel: 071-378 0296

RELIGIOUS SOCIETY OF FRIENDS
Quaker Home Service, Friends House, 73 Euston Road, London, NW1 2BJ
Tel: 071-387 3601

REFUGEE COUNCIL
Bondway House, 3 Bondway, London, SW8 1SJ
Tel: 071-582 6922

RETURNED VOLUNTEER ACTION (RVA)
1, Amwell Street, London, EC1R 1UL
Tel: 071-278 0804

SAVE THE CHILDREN FUND (SCF)
Mary Datchelor House, 17 Grove Lane, Camberwell, London, SE5 8SP
Tel: 071-703 5400

SCIAF
5 Oswald Street, Glasgow, G1 4QR
Tel: 041-221 4447

SCOTTISH CHURCHES ACTION FOR WORLD DEVELOPMENT (SCAWD)
41 George IV Bridge, Edinburgh, EH1 1EL
Tel: 031-225 1772

SCOTTISH EDUCATION AND ACTION FOR DEVELOPMENT (SEAD)
23 Castle Street, Edinburgh, EH2 3DN
Tel: 031-225 6550

SIGHT SAVERS
191, Heywards Heath, West Sussex, RH16 4YF
Tel: 0444-412424.

STUDENT CHRISTIAN MOVEMENT (SCM)
186 St. Pauls Road, Balsall Heath, Birmingham BI2 8LZ
Tel: 021 440 3000

SURVIVAL INTERNATIONAL
310 Edgware Rd, London, W2 1DY
Tel: 071-723 5535

TEAR FUND
100 Church Road, Teddington, Middx, TW11 8QE
Tel: 081-977 9144

THIRD WORLD FIRST
232 Cowley Road, Oxford, OX4 1UH
Tel: 0865-245678

TOURISM CONCERN
Froebel College, Roehampton Lane, London, SW15 5PU
Tel: 081- 878 9053

TRADE UNION INTERNATIONAL RESEARCH AND EDUCATION GROUP (TUIREG)
Ruskin College, Walton Street, Oxford, OX1 2HE
Tel: 0865-54599

TRAIDCRAFT PLC.
Kingsway, Team Valley Trading Estate, Gateshead, NE11 0NE
Tel: 091-491 0591

UNITED NATIONS ASSOCIATION (UNA)
3 Whitehall Court, London, SW1A 2EL
Tel: 071-930 2931

UNITED NATIONS HIGH COMMISSIONER FOR REFUGEES
36 Westminster Palace Gardens, Artillery Row, London, SW1P 1RR
Tel: 071-222 3065

UNITED REFORMED CHURCH YOUTH OFFICE
86 Tavistock Place, London, WC1H 9RT
Tel: 071-916 2020

UNITED SOCIETY FOR THE PROPAGATION OF THE GOSPEL (USPG)
Partnership House, 157 Waterloo Road, London, SE1 8XA
Tel: 071-928 8681

VACATION WORK
9, Park End Street, Oxford, OX1 1HJ
Tel: 0865-241978

VOLUNTARY SERVICE OVERSEAS (VSO)
317, Putney Bridge Road, London, SW15 2PG
Tel: 081-780 2266

WORLD DEVELOPMENT MOVEMENT (WDM)
25 Beehive Place, London, SW9 7QR
Tel: 071-737 6215

WORLD WIDE FUND FOR NATURE
Panda House, Weyside Park, Godalming, Surrey, GU7 1XR
Tel: 0483-426444

Y CARE INTERNATIONAL
640 Forest Rd, London, E17 3DZ
Tel: 081-520 5599

YOUTH EXCHANGE CENTRE
British Council, 10 Spring Gardens, London, SW1A 2BN
Tel: 071-389 4030